Whitetail
ADVANTAGE

Understand Deer Behavior
for Hunting Success

Dr. David Samuel & Bob Zaiglin

Published by

kp **krause publications**

An Imprint of F+W Publications

700 East State Street • Iola, WI 54990-0001
715-445-2214 • 888-457-2873
www.krausebooks.com

Our toll-free number to place an order or obtain
a free catalog is (800) 258-0929.

Library of Congress Control Number: 2008925076

ISBN-13: 978-0-89689-681-9

ISBN-10: 0-89689-681-1

Designed by Heidi Bittner-Zastrow

Edited by Derrek Sigler

Printed in China

DEDICATION

Over the years I've been away from home a fair amount, either bowhunting or serving on board and committees pushing education and the values of wildlife and wildlife management. My wife Cathy made this possible and thus, this book is dedicated to my biggest supporter and the best helpmate that a husband ever had.

I also want to dedicate this to all the hunters and friends who have given me strength and support during the recent times as I've dealt with a serious health issue. Your continued prayers and support sustain me. You make me proud to be a member of a hunting community that comes together in times of need. God bless you all.

Dr. David Samuel

I dedicate this book to my wife Jan. For 29 years she has been my principal supporter and source of inspiration. Secondly, I would like to thank all my fellow deer biologists who constitute the number one source of research on whitetail deer—the Southeast Deer Study Group.

Bob Zaiglin

CONTENTS

F O R E W O R D
by Dr. Dave Samuel

I've spent my life hunting and studying wildlife. For 30 years I was a wildlife professor at West Virginia University. While there my graduate students conducted a number of research projects involving white-tailed deer, but my love for whitetails started long before my professorial career. I've been fascinated with them since I was a kid, in fact I vividly remember my first day hunting (age 12) and seeing that first deer up close and personal.

My twin brother and I went on our first hunt (squirrels) with my father on State Game Lands near Rainsburg, Pennsylvania. For some strange unremembered reason, that year the season did not open until 9 AM. We arrived about an hour before that legal hunting time, so my brother and I went for a short walk near the parked car. We hadn't gone one hundred yards when we spotted a gray squirrel, and picked out a log to sit on. Some rustling

Dr. Dave with a Coues deer. Coues are a hard-to-hunt subspecies of whitetail found in the Southwest.

leaves caused me to turn to the right, and there, not twenty yards away was an eight-point buck.

The hearts of two twelve-year-old boys could be heard beating yards away. As Aldo Leopold once wrote, any woods-loving boy whose heart doesn't jump out of his chest at the sight of a buck that close isn't quite normal. He walked closer and soon was only fifteen feet away, feeding on red maple twigs. When he winded us, snorted, and ran, my brother and I were left with an indelible image that is still vivid 55 years later. To this day the magic and excitement I felt that morning has been the defining reason I hunt—to feel that rush, the thundering heartbeat, the shortness of breath and the tingling feeling of being so close to such a majestic creature. So began my first hunting day in the woods.

While a professor and bowhunter, I also started another career—outdoor writing. I just completed my 36th year as Conservation Editor of Bowhunter magazine and have also written the whitetail column for Petersen's Bowhunting. I also presently write the "Know Whitetails" column for the Whitetail Journal and do the "Ask Dr. Dave About Whitetail Deer" for www.sportsmansguide.com.

Samuel's Iowa buck.
Look at that mass!

Zaiglin's 1987 buck
gross scored 184 inches.

Zaiglin's first drop-tine buck, taken in Mexico, was awarded first place-Mexico division by the Freer Muy Grande contest in 1989.

While a professor, wildlife researcher, and outdoor writer, I studied deer in the field, observed them from my treestand, and read hundreds of scientific articles published in wildlife journals on whitetails. For many years I attended the Southeast Deer Study Group Meeting, an annual event where the top deer biologists present the latest information on these great animals. More recently I attend the annual convention of the Quality Deer Management Association.

I used the information garnered from the above to develop talks for deer seminars, banquets, programs for church game dinners, and stories for magazines. I discovered that hunters were very interested in the latest scientific information, when presented in a way that would help their hunting success. Information included such things as: at what age do bucks have their largest antlers? Does the moon affect buck movements? Does rattling really work? Do older bucks do all the mating? How effective are mock scrapes? Do yearling bucks that disperse ever return to their original home range? How do

I find a deer's core home range, and why is it important? etc., etc.

Invariably after a presentation, hunters would ask me, "Where then can I get all this neat information?" I'd then explain that I got some from scientific journals, some from talking to deer biologists, and some at the Southeast Deer Study Group Meeting or at the Quality Deer Management Association's annual convention. I'd then tell them that there was no one place where that information was available. Not until now.

Three years ago, I realized that a book covering the latest deer research, especially research that provided clues to making a hunter more successful, was needed. And thus, the idea for this book was born. When it came time to start this project, I realized that I couldn't do this alone. First, I didn't have enough good photographs to do such a book. Second, I needed someone who worked with deer, understood deer, and could write about deer, and who could help pull this book together.

Dr. Dave with a P&Y buck.

Enter Bob Zaiglin. I'd known Bob for many years, since he had been a student in my wildlife classes at West Virginia University. I always liked him. Most everyone does. After graduation, he went on to get a Master's Degree in wildlife from Texas A & I University (now named Texas A & M University at Kingsville), working under famous deer researcher, Dr. Charles DeYoung and famed wildlife manager Al Brothers. He then became a Field Research Coordinator at Stephen F. Austin State University in Nacogdoches, Texas working under another whitetail deer authority, Dr. James C. Kroll.

In 1979 Bob accepted the position of Wildlife Manager for Valley View Cattle on the Lochridge Ranch located south of Athens, Texas. He remained at Lochridge Ranch until 1983 when he became Wildlife Manager for Harrison Interests, Ltd. Bob managed nearly 175,000 acres of premiere Texas wildlife habitat, including the 106,000-acre Piloncillo Ranch located in Dimmit, Webb, and LaSalle Counties, Texas. Since fall of 2004, Bob has

Zaiglin's second Boone and Crockett buck taken in 2001.

been Department Head and wildlife management instructor at Southwest Texas Junior College where he established the first and only two-year applied science degree program in wildlife management in Texas. He also owns and operates Zaiglin's Wildlife Resource Management, a highly successful consulting firm.

Bob has been a field editor for the Texas Trophy Hunter Magazine since its inception in 1975. He has been the white-tailed editor for Texas Outdoors Journal since 1993, and southern field editor for Deer & Deer Hunting since 1999. He lives in Uvalde, Texas with his wife, Jan, of 29 years. As a hunter, he has taken a number of outstanding whitetails, two of which are in the all time Boone and Crockett record book.

One short note about reading this book. In some chapters you will note that we use the word "I" rather than "we." I did a fair amount of the writing, but Bob edited and added to everything I wrote, and he also wrote several chapters, which I edited and added to as well. I quickly realized that to use "we" throughout became awkward. So, you will see the "I" and "we" terms interspersed throughout, and that can mean either Dave or Bob, or both of us. Sometimes, for clarity, you will see either Bob's initials (RZ) or mine (DS) following the word "I." Enough on that; this book is our joint effort.

What we have tried to do with this book is to include the latest information on deer. Rather than cover everything, we've tried to focus on topics that are timely, and of interest to you, the hunter. Note: this is not a "how to hunt" book. Rather it contains tons of information that will explain why and what you saw from your treestand. We hope that it is a book where you will read a paragraph and a light will go on, as you realize why you saw what you saw at your favorite hunting location this past season.

My analogy is that you can drive a car even if you don't know the intricacies of how the parts make it run, but you will be a safer, better, driver if you know the parts and how they work. My good friend, and great whitetail bowhunter, Barry Wensel, puts it this way. "This is a piece of the puzzle." He is right. Understanding whitetails is a life long passion for many of us. If we worked at it 365 days a year for our entire life, we would not be able to put all the pieces of the puzzle together. In fact, we wouldn't even know what all the "pieces" are, much less fit them together so that we fully understood what whitetails do, why they do it, when they do it, etc.

Hopefully this book will at least help you make sense of the things you see in the field. In so doing they will help you map out your hunting strategy, an evolving strategy that changes from day to day and year to year as you learn more about this great animal.

What you will read is a summary of research done by deer biologists; a summary of things we think will benefit hunters. Most is about the deer, but there are a few chapters that are about hunting in general. For example, we've covered that latest information on Chronic Wasting Disease, because you are hearing so much about that disease. We've also put together a short chapter on trophy hunting, simply because some hunters and many non-hunters have a misconception about what it is. And the last chapter on the future of hunting is something we both felt was important and worth including. We hope you agree.

Putting this book together has been a big job, but fun. Writing about the greatest animal on the continent was a pleasure for me, and for Bob. Working with Derrek Sigler and the other folks at Krause Publications has been a pleasure and we thank them for putting up with us.

We know there are things we missed. And we know it isn't perfect by any stretch, but we hope that as you finish each chapter, you will say to yourself, "Gee, I didn't know that. Pretty neat stuff."

The whitetail unquestionably reigns as the most popular big game animal in North America.

CHAPTER 1

Some Whitetail History

O f all the wild species that graze on this continent, deer just might be the most adaptable. Consider that they have the widest longitudinal range of any large hoofed animal in North America. We find deer from northern Canada and they continue to move even further north in Alberta, to South America where they continue their southerly range expansion.

They also have the most genetic diversity of all large grazers, which is another reason the adaptable deer is so widespread. Relative to deer numbers, we've come full circle as there are now almost as many deer than there was in early colonial times. Early settlers ate venison and also sold hundreds of thousands of deer hides to Europe. Throughout the 1800's Americans ate venison. Loggers, railroad builders, restaurants in major eastern cities consumed huge amounts of venison. Without game laws, deer numbers plummeted from an estimated 20 million to less than half a million. But deer habitat changed as many forests were cut and land converted to agriculture. These activities created food for deer and with the help of federal legislation, deer numbers rebounded.

It's a cycle we've seen repeated over the years. Indeed deer numbers run in cycles, dictated by man's activity. Cutting forests initially leads to lots of food for deer, which leads to high deer numbers. But as new seedlings grow away from the deer into pole stage timber, deer foods disappear and numbers again drop. History shows that when deer numbers decline, hunters blame state wildlife agencies. What has happened in our home state of Pennsylvania (your authors were both born there) is fairly typical. The Game Commission protected does to allow deer numbers to rise. Then in the 1970's Pennsylvania and other state game agencies realized that deer numbers required more control than buck seasons could provide. They attempted to implement antlerless harvests, and hunters went ballistic. Clearly years of protecting does had "trained" hunters to believe that harvesting does was just not a good thing. At the same time thousands of small family farms were abandoned, establishing vegetation desired by deer. Protection of does and

Adaptable as rabbits, deer live and flourish right alongside of man.

Modern day sportsmen now employ luxury deer blinds.

*The elaborate top-drive rigs common in Texas
in search of a trophy buck.*

*Here, wildlife technicians use a
helicopter to relocate deer.*

habitat changes probably led to the deer explosion that started in the 1980's.

During the deer boom of the 80's and 90's, the millions of hunters that entertained the sport thought it was "the norm" to see 30 or more deer per day. These high deer numbers and a growing group of hunters who felt this was a good thing, created a major problem for state agencies and a hot biological-political situation that continues today.

There are now an estimated 30 million deer inhabiting the United States, living in all conceivable habitats. They do well in forests, fields, wetlands, mountains, valleys, wilderness, and cities. The economic impact of deer hunting and deer viewing is huge. With such high deer numbers come negatives such as crop damage, diseases, and auto/deer collisions leading to huge financial losses and some loss of human life.

In recent years, along with the growth of deer herds, we've seen major changes in deer hunting. When your authors started deer hunting, it was learning pretty much through trial and error. In the past ten years there has been an explosion of information available to hunters. For example, Bowhunter Education was merely a blip on the map back in 1971; today it's huge. We now have "How To" articles by the dozen, "How To" videos, books, television shows, the Internet, and seminars everywhere. The amount of material available on equipment, hunting, and the animals we pursue is incredible. Equipment changes are endless. We've got plastic fletchings, drop away rests, carbon arrows, expandable broadheads, rangefinders, ground blinds, light-enhancing scopes, ATV's, an explosion of muzzleloaders, etc. The endless list goes on. Clothes have also changed with scent-reducing apparel, quiet rain gear, better gloves, facemasks, cold weather clothes, much better boots and shoes... Just look through a Cabela's catalog and you'll see what I mean.

Knowledge of the deer they hunt and how to improve antler quality has become important to deer hunting managers "who make a management decision each and every time they pull the trigger".

Deer propagation is now considered one of the most rapidly growing industries in rural America according to a study published by Texas A&M University (2007).

Hunting has also changed. Sportsmen have less access to private lands, more leasing, evolution of quality deer management, much more baiting, 3-D target shoots, a great increase in raising and hunting deer in confinement, the explosion of Chronic Wasting Disease (yes, CWD was in this country in the late 1960's, but numbers were so low there was no concern. In fact, most folks did not know it was around). We've got higher license fees, more demand for non-resident western state permits, and urban deer problems.

Thirty years ago, anti-hunters were barely visible, and antler restrictions meant that you could only shoot spikes with 3-inch antlers. My how times have changed. Oh yes, one other relatively recent change over the past 50 years is the amount of deer research going on. We learn more about whitetails every day. Read on, because presenting the latest facts based on deer research is what this book is all about.

A deer's nose (its olfactory system) is constantly employed to identify food and danger as well as other deer.

CHAPTER 2

A Buck's Nose Knows

How many times have you heard this story? The hunter walks to his tree stand before daylight on a cold November morning. He sees a few deer, but nothing close enough for a shot. But he knows there is a big buck in the area, so he hangs in there until noon. It's cold, and he is tired and hungry so he departs and doesn't return to that stand until the following evening.

Knowing that deer have great noses, he notes the wind and enters the stand on a different path than the one he took the morning before. With great anticipation he settles in for the wait. An hour before dark he hears a deer walking in the leaves. It is a dandy buck and headed right for him.

Just out of range, the buck stops, and puts his nose to the ground. He doesn't blow out of there, but just turns and quickly walks away. The wind was perfect, yet the deer never got closer than sixty or seventy yards. The hunter grudgingly gets down from the stand and walks to the spot where the deer turned away. He discovers that the buck had just intersected the trail he'd walked in on the day before.

Whoa! A deer's nose knows.

Human activity forces mature bucks to flee—a response acquired early in life that is repeated each time it detects the scent of a human.

There have been estimates that a deer can smell as much as 10,000 times better than we can. Others say it is less than that, but what really matters, and what every hunter knows, is that they can definitely smell better than we can. They can smell better by a long shot too.

Deer use their nose to survive. Their sense of smell is the major way deer detect predators, find food, and it helps them communicate with other deer during breeding season. They use their nose at scrapes, overhanging limbs, at buck rubs, and around does to help them cue to what is happening before and during the rut. In essence, a deer survives by its nose, and they rely on their sense of smell for everything.

We will never fully understand how a deer uses its sense of smell, but there is new research on how mice and humans process odors and it may give us some real clues as to how deer smell as well. Knowing how deer use their highly tuned sense of smell will show you why it is so important to stay as scent free as possible. If you aren't sure about this, then read on. What follows should convince you that being able to detect your odor is something that deer can do extremely well.

In 2004, two researchers got the Nobel Prize in Physiology for their work on how humans detect odors. What they learned was most interesting. Humans have a small patch of odor receptor cells inside the nose. (This gets a bit complex, but don't go away.) These odor receptor cells make proteins that allow the detection of different odors. What determines the proteins that these cells make? Genes. Genes code these proteins, so the ability for all mammals including humans and deer to smell, is tied to genes. Each protein in each odor receptor cell can allow mice to smell between one and three different odors. Since mice have at least 1000 of these genes, they can potentially smell as many as 3,000 different odors.

Humans have only 300 of these genes, meaning they can smell as many as 900 odors. We don't know how many genes deer have, but they definitely have way more than we do. One would guess that deer have at least 500 proteins and the genes to create them, and if each allows them to smell between one and three odors, they could potentially smell 1,500 different odors.

Though that is important, the next finding by these scientists is the kicker. These different odor receptor cells take in various odors, and send that information to the brain where patterns are formed.

Here is what the scientific research report quoted on this formation of patterns by inhaling different odors, "we (meaning humans) can consciously experience the smell of a lilac flower in the spring and recall this olfactory memory at other times."

"A unique odor can trigger distinct memories..."

So a unique odor can trigger distinct memories. Let's put this in deer language. We have odors coming into the deer's nose, hitting the receptor cells that have these proteins created by genes that allow odors to go to the brain. There the deer forms patterns based on everything that was going on when it smelled a certain odor or odors. Now how does this all work to a deer's advantage?

A buck employs its second nose, the vomeronasal gland, to detect estrus in a doe.
Knowledge of this behavior insures the hunter when a deer is actually focused
on something other than danger.

Odor particles adhere to a deer's nose more efficiently when it is wet, thus they instinctively lick their noses to maintain moisture. This is commonly seen during the rut.

Let's say a deer walks into an alfalfa field. Of course the deer sees the field, and it smells the alfalfa. That deer has been to the field many times before, so there is a pattern already in the brain that says, "I see the field and I smell alfalfa, so it is time to chow down." Odors create patterns and these patterns determine where a deer will eat. If the deer walks in a certain direction and smells an odor that is part of a pattern created a month before, then that tells him to continue in that direction and he/she will find food. It might be alfalfa, it might be acorns, or it might be brassica. The pattern was created and the deer reacts.

What if a buck runs into a dog and that dog chases him? The deer smelled the dog and then gets chased, and that is now a pattern in the deer's brain. Next time he smells a dog, he will run away. If he is a young buck, then he might stand around a few seconds after seeing the second dog, and he may then get chased. Ah ha! The pattern is reinforced, so the third time he sees a dog, he is gone. Someone once told me that a buck isn't all that smart, he just has great reaction time. True, and he is reacting to learned patterns in the brain tied to odors.

This whole pattern thing works the same when deer have encounters with hunters. What odors might a deer get around a human? Cigarettes, perspiration, clothes, gasoline, aftershave, you name it. If a deer encounters those odors while living in a state park where there is no hunting, then it may not form a negative pattern. In fact, the deer may form a neutral pattern. Nothing bad happened when he smelled those odors, so the deer became accustomed to the presence of humans. The odors are part of a pattern that did not result in anything negative for the deer, so they do not react. In essence they became relatively tame.

Repeated hunts from the same blind reduces hunter success because of human scent remaining at the site.

But if there is a negative human encounter, associated with perspiration odor, or cigarette odor, or any human odor, that deer forms a pattern. The older the deer, the more reinforcement he/she got, so the reaction may well be instant.

Let's go back to the buck that smelled the hunter's boots or shoes on the trail he took to the tree stand. Apparently that buck had an earlier negative encounter with a human. He got the odor, something negative happened, and a pattern was formed. That pattern was there when he got a whiff of humans, so he left in a hurry.

So, all human-related odors are stored away in a deer's brain and the patterns generated by odors are there as long as that deer lives. If deer are around farms, people, with no negative encounters (i.e. no dogs chase them, no hunters, etc.), then the patterns they store won't result in flight. However, in most deer country, those human-related odors are negative for the deer, and they react by fleeing.

Deer will lick their noses all the time, especially bucks during the rut, because odor particles stick to a deer's nose better when it is wet. So wet weather may also enhance the ability of a deer to recognize an odor. I love to bowhunt on mornings when there is a mist in the air. But be aware that a deer's sense of smell may well be enhanced at such a time.

We've learned that deer smell better than we thought, and we now know that they put things that happen to them, plus the odors, into patterns that determine their behavior. The question then is what can we do about it? The answer is simple. Reduce your odor any way possible. There are all kinds of products out there that can help reduce odor, such as scent-free soaps, deodorants, scent-reducing clothes, scent-reducing sprays, etc. You can also keep your odors from clothing by keeping them clean, placing them in scent-proof bags or containers, putting your hunting clothes on outside, and do not get overheated while going to your stand.

Why is it that the best chance to take a big buck is often the first time you sit in a new stand? Odor. Reusing a stand means more odors in the area. Let's say you sat a stand three evenings in a row. If an older buck comes in downwind, and gets your odor, you may never see him. Many of our best hunters will tell you that controlling scent and watching the wind is critical. This is especially true for bowhunters who have to get close to harvest a deer.

A guide I hunted with in Montana many years ago was the one who told me that deer are not smart; they just have great reaction time. I never fully understood that until I found the above research. That reaction time is all about odor and patterns formed in reaction to odors. Deer can react to those patterns in milliseconds. The older the deer, the more those patterns are reinforced and the better the reaction time.

The bottom line here is that you need to take all the steps possible to eliminate your odor, because a buck's nose knows.

Hunter: *It is neat to learn all this, but what's new here? I mean, I already knew they had a great nose.*

Dave/Bob: *True, and the only things we've given you that you probably didn't know were details on how a deer's sense of smell works. What's new is a bit scary, in that we now know that deer can detect hundreds of different odors, put them together into a pattern in their brain, and remember that forever. What the information in this chapter does is reinforce the importance of scent control.*

Hunter: *So, is there anything I can do to eliminate my human odor to deer?*

Dave/Bob: *Actually you cannot eliminate your odor. But you can assuredly reduce it by doing all of the things listed above (wash often with scent-free soap, keep your clothes in scent-free bags, stay away from household odors, etc.). In fact, you can't be too detailed in your daily hunting regime when it comes to controlling your scent.*

Sidenote: Parts of this chapter adapted from Dr Dave's "Know Whitetail" column in the *Whitetail Journal*.

A deer's ability to see color really became of interest to sportsmen when states initiated laws requiring gun hunters to wear fluorescent orange clothing.

CHAPTER 3

The Eyes Have It

The whitetail survives because of it's senses; smell, hearing, sight, touch, and taste. If you analyzed the importance of each of these senses, the top one that aids survival would probably be smell, followed by hearing. We list sight as third because, relative to sight, deer do have some limitations. Then again they have components of vision that give them distinct advantages for living and surviving in the wild.

Let's start with some basics. Vision begins when light enters the eye and is absorbed by the photoreceptor cells (cones and rods) located in the retina. Objects don't have color. They just reflect light of a particular wavelength that our brain perceives as color. Color vision is the capacity to distinguish the wavelengths of the objects when it is reflected into our eyes. Let's also add something on rods and cones - a refresher from your middle school science class. On the back of the eye is the retina and it contains rods and cones. Rods allow one to see black and white; cones allow one to see color.

We have lots of cones and these receptors are sensitive to three wavelengths (long—allows us to perceive reds, middle—allows us to perceive greens, and short—allows us to perceive blues). From those three wavelengths we see all colors. Deer on the other hand, have lots of rods, and some cones. The cones allow them to see color only when there is sunlight,

Some researchers believe that deer see red and orange colors as shades of gray or yellow. However, peak sensitivity is in the blue range, thus they see blue extremely well. Based on this fact or knowing this, blue jeans would not be considered ideal hunter attire.

while the rods allow them to see when it is dark. In essence then, deer see color in the day and cannot detect color at night. At dawn and dusk, both the rods and cones are working so the deer, relative to their vision, are in a transition period.

Of course the age-old question hunters have bantered about for many years is whether deer can see color. Originally the controversy stemmed from a hunter safety issue when years ago states started requiring deer gun hunters to wear a certain amount of fluorescent orange clothing. Hunters were concerned that wearing the bright orange would make them as visible to deer as it did to other hunters. For years we believed that deer simply saw everything as black or white, because anatomists studying the eye of deer found lots of rods. Now we know better. Today, researchers believe that deer can see color, though not as we do. Research done by Drs. Karl Miller and Gino D'Angelo at the University of Georgia, in cooperation with scientists at the University of California Santa Barbara, showed that deer do have lots of rods, but they also have some cones in their retina that provide the ability to perceive some color.

Deer have fewer cones then we do, and thus are only sensitive to two wavelengths; middle—allows them to perceive greens and yellows, and short—allows them to perceive blues. In essence they have poor color vision, especially in the longer wavelengths (the part of the spectrum that allows us to orange and red). Deer do not discern those longer wavelength colors well at all.

Some researchers believe that deer see reds and orange colors as shades of gray or yellow. They do see better in the middle wavelength colors, such as green, and in the shorter wavelengths, such as blue. In fact, deer see the greens and blues better than we do. For deer, peak sensitivity is in the blue range; they see blue very well so wearing blue jeans might not be a good idea when you are hunting.

Research has speculated that deer see UV wavelengths really well (and we don't see them at all because we have a pigment to block out destructive UV light. UV light would also harm the eyes of deer if they lived as long as we do). This has led to the speculation that using detergents that have UV brighteners makes it easy for deer to see our clothes. Does this really happen? We don't know, but the science certainly leads one to think that it is a distinct possibility. Atsko makes Sport-Wash laundry detergent and U-V-Killer Spray to keep clothes UV-brightener free. These products definitely reduce UV glow. Should you use them? That isn't our call, but why not? Why take the chance?

A great advantage deer have comes from the added number of rods they have in the retina. These allow them to see very well in low light. The ability to see in low light is accentuated because they have a tapetum lucidum located behind the retina. This membrane reflects light back through the retina, increasing the amount of light available to the eye, enhancing night vision. When you shine a light in the eye of a deer at night, you get that reflection because deer have this tapetum. Drs. Miller and D'Angelo showed that more of the tapetum is found in the upper region of the eye, and they then speculate that this allows the deer to better see reflected light from the ground. Just another adaptation deer have to allow them to see in very low light.

Their low-light vision is also enhanced because they can open their pupil three times wider than we can. This allows the eye to admit a lot more light. Add to that the fact that they have lots of rods, which are the receptors needed for low light conditions. One researcher went so far as to compare our ability to see orange with the deer's ability to see in low light. The conclusion was that in the very short wavelengths (in the UV range), where we can't see those UV colors at all, deer can see them, and they can see them better than we see blaze orange. It's scary how well deer see in low light.

This morning I watched two different hunting shows on television that talked about how you shouldn't bother to hunt during the full moon because the deer could see at night and thus feed all night. Think about this for a minute. Deer do a lot of moving around at night, so through evolution they have eyes that function at night. If they didn't, they would bed all night and feed all day. But that isn't the case.

In chapter 9 we'll present some scientific data from South Texas that shows no relationship to deer moving and the full moon. Other data does show a relationship, but even so, believing that moonlight allows them to be more active and feed more at night than when there is no full moon is a bit silly. When it is totally dark, with no moon at all, deer do very well at night. They aren't out there stumbling around, walking into trees, because their eyes have a number of adaptations that allow them to see extremely well in low light. The full moon isn't much of an advantage to them, if any. They do not need it to see. Now maybe the light from the full moon plays a role in determining when they rut (we'll leave that for chapter 9), but they sure don't need moonlight to see at night.

The eyes of deer are positioned in a manner which enhances their ability to scan a wide area.

Here are some other things about deer vision to ponder.

The eyes of deer are not as close together as ours are. Predators tend to have eyes close together giving them better binocular vision. Deer, however, have eyes further apart, which gives them the ability to cover a lot of ground with their eyes. The added rods also give deer an extraordinary ability to detect movement. What hunters need to take away from all this is that movement is what does us in. Movement. Movement. Do not move. When on stand, do not make unnecessary movements.

Consider the following relative to how well deer see in the day. Researchers at the University of Georgia focused on how their visual system affects deer behavior. These researchers found that deer have 80 percent less acuity than humans (Aha, finally something that might give us an edge over deer). Here is why.

Humans have something called an optic fovea that is located in the central region of the retina. That area has many, many cones and only

Deer can get used to an object such as a deer blind but acutely detect movement from within, erasing its benefits. Hunters must be cautious when moving even inside a blind.

humans and primates have an optic fovea. It is responsible for sharp central vision and allows us to focus on one spot. When we focus on one spot (as you are now, reading these words) things in the periphery are blurred. Stop reading and just focus on this word. Note, the further you are from the focused word, the blurrier the image. Being able to see that word very clearly is called visual acuity. (When you get your eyes tested and you look at letters on the screen, you are really having your visual acuity measured). Ours is very good, but that isn't the case for deer. They do not have an optic fovea that gives them lots of photoreceptors in one spot on the retina.

Rather deer have a band of photoreceptors (mostly cones) across the retina. This allows a deer to scan a wide field of view all at once, without moving their eyes. Now deer don't have as many cones in this narrow band as we do. Thus, their visual acuity is not as good as ours.

Thus, when you have a deer standing at 80 yards facing in your direction, but not looking at you, they will see any movement. Add to this the fact that deer have rod photoreceptors that allow great vision in low light and one starts to understand why we get spotted. One other thing, with the wide field of view, deer have reduced depth perception. They can spot your movement, but may not readily know how far away you are.

The key then, relative to deer vision, is their ability to detect movement. Keep these different vision capabilities in mind as you observe deer in the field and as you tune your hunting strategies, because when it comes to a deer's vision, the eyes have it.

Deer lack sharp central vision thus they cannot focus on one spot, an advantage afforded hunters capable of remaining relatively motionless.

Hunter: *It seems to me that from what you say, deer see lots of shades of gray or yellow. In fact, for most colors, they are seeing either shades of yellow or gray. Is that right?*

Dave/Bob: *Yes, that is correct.*

Hunter: *They also apparently can see very well in the blue range. Does this mean that wearing blue jeans makes me more visible to deer?*
Dave/Bob: *Yes, that is probably correct.*

Hunter: *And since they can see really well in the blue range, using detergents with brighteners puts more blue-range UV colors on my clothes and thus makes it easier to be seen by deer. Is that right?*

Dave/Bob: *Well, it is a little more complicated than that, but in essence, that is apparently true.*

Hunter: *Knowing all this, how does this impact the clothing I should wear when I hunt?*

Dave/Bob: *First, the blaze orange color we see is not blaze orange for deer. It is probably a shade of gray (unless you wash it in detergents using brighteners. In that case, blaze orange will be seen as a blue color). Second, clothes of one color, orange for example, will be a blob of gray to the deer. Big blobs of color are probably easier to see by a deer, than a camo pattern. Deer do not see well in the longer and middle wavelengths. That part of the spectrum is oranges, greens, yellows, browns, and reds. Thus, camo patterns of greens, browns, grays, etc. are not seen the same by deer, but they would still be a mix for the deer, rather than a big blob of a gray shade.*

Hunter: *It seems to me that we have two things here relative to a deer's vision. First is the ability to see really well in low light, much better than we can. Second, the movement issue you discussed. Does wearing camo reduce the ability of a deer to see movement?*

Dave/Bob: *Relative to twisting your body while on stand, it may well do that. But if you flip up your arm, even in camo, you enhance the chance of being seen by a deer, even one that is not looking directly at you. Combine that with their ability to see better at dawn and dusk, and you start to understand that curbing your movement is critical to escaping the eyes of a deer.*

Contrary to popular belief, deer can and will look up.

Fawns are easy to distinguish; however, nubbin bucks in the fall are sometimes challenging to identify and are harvested as does.

CHAPTER 4

Aging Deer
on the Hoof

The concept of quality deer management originated in Texas. It continues to impact the hunter experience throughout the U.S. The ramifications on other species such as mule deer and elk are equally as strong. Large antlers have always fascinated hunters. The fact that basic management techniques employed by sportsmen can increase the availability of quality animals makes for an exciting time in the hunting world.

A quality hunting experience, however, requires more than a trophy set of antlers. It includes all the prehunt preparation such as locating that ideal piece of deer turf, up to and including staying physically fit in order to cover that extra mile or withstand variable temperatures. The fair chase pursuit of the animal is paramount to the experience in order for the sportsman to feel confident that skill was required in order to capitalize on outwitting a cunning rare animal. Above all else is with whom the experience is shared. With these requirements met, walking up on a trophy-caliber animal represents the final touch often expressed as "icing on the cake."

Sportsmen are cognizant of the fact that antlers increase in size with age. Depending on their expectations, they are often willing to allow immature bucks the opportunity to reach their optimum antler growing years. Not all deer, however, have to survive six years in order to satisfy a high percentage of sportsmen.

For example, in Pennsylvania, up until recent changes added antler restrictions, ninety-plus percent of the yearling bucks were harvested annually. Thus, few hunters got the opportunity to see a two-year-old buck, and a three-year-old buck would have been considered a phenomenon. In this situation, a quality hunting experience could be developed by simply allowing bucks to reach their second year knowing that a few would enter the three-year-old category.

Antler size and characteristics vary on a regional basis, but restraint can dictate just how big those antlers get. In reality, hunters are the managers of this resource because each time a trigger is pulled, a management decision is made. Unlike bass fishing, there is no catch-and-release scenario. In order to reduce the harvest of young bucks, hunters must be able to estimate the age of bucks in the wild.

Estimating the age of a deer on the hoof is extremely challenging

It takes time to critique the rack and physical attributes of a buck, but time is often limited. Aging deer on the hoof remains an educated guess. Even seasoned hunters make mistakes. Experience remains paramount to one's ability to estimate the age of live deer.

When attempting to age deer in the bush, the nutritional status of the animals must also be considered. For example, in South Texas, periodic drought negatively impacts antler development due to the sub-par range conditions they create. Thus sportsmen employing antler size criteria to complement their age estimate in this region must pay particular attention to weather conditions during the spring and summer antler-growing periods. In dry years with poor range conditions, average antler size will drop significantly, resulting in underestimating a buck's age. Worse yet, prime-aged bucks can be harvested because hunters consider the animals inferior (antler-size-wise) for their age and remove them for what is often referred to as management bucks, whereas if passed over, these bucks could develop exceptional antlers in subsequent years under ideal conditions.

Three characteristics are employed to estimate age of live bucks—antler size, body characteristics, and behavior. The following is an overview of characteristics that can be employed in the field to age whitetails on the hoof.

Yearlings: 1½-year-old bucks

A yearling buck can be described as a doe with antlers. Ears are semi-pointed at the terminal end, and the nose is well defined and square in appearance. Their legs appear long and thin because their body is slim. Yearlings will not develop a swollen neck or the muscular features of older bucks. Although fawns rub tarsal glands, a yearling's tarsals remain small and

A yearling can be defined as a doe with antlers.

Note the more pointed ear tip of the yearling.

tan in color. In the relaxed or semi-alert position, the tip-to-tip measurement between the ears is approximately 14 inches. Seldom will a yearling buck exhibit an outside antler spread over 14 inches.

The number of antler points is not a reliable feature when estimating age. This is especially true in nutritionally strong deer habitat and in supplementally fed herds where yearlings commonly produce six, eight, or even 10-point antlers.

Two-year-old bucks are obviously larger than yearlings, but their legs remain long in proportion to their body.

2½-year-old bucks*

At two years of age, antlers are not large, but can make you take a second look. They are larger than yearlings, but their legs remain long in proportion to their body. Their belly remains firm with no sag whatsoever. During the rut, neck swelling is minimal. The tarsal glands begin to get darker in color, but obviously less than older males. When observed broadside, the head appears elongated.

*Descriptions list the age as 1½, 2½, 3½, etc., rather than 2, 3, 4, etc., because they are 1½, 2½, 3½ years of age in the hunting season, when you are attempting to age them on the hoof. The photos were not all taken in the hunting season, so for simplicity these are labeled 2, 3, 4, etc. years of age.

At 3 years, muscling absent in two-year-olds becomes obvious; however, a distinction between the chest and neck exists.

Some define the appearance of a three-year-old as that of a well-conditioned race horse.

3½-year-old bucks

Middle-aged bucks portray a muscled neck and deeper chest, yet a distinct junction between the neck and shoulder exists. Some describe their appearance as that of a well-conditioned racehorse. Muscling absent in 2½-year-olds begins to become obvious in the third year. Their chest begins to appear as large as their rump. Antler spread is often outside the ears and on quality habitat impressive antlers can develop. For inexperienced individuals, three-year-olds are often mistaken for mature bucks.

At four years of age, the animal is muscled throughout, but their stomach remains semi-taut and their ears appear somewhat rounded at the tips.

4½-year-old bucks

Bucks mature at four years of age and lose the racehorse appearance. The obvious junction between the neck and the shoulders fades away as the neck becomes firmly muscled, appearing almost as large as the chest. The animal is muscled throughout, but their stomach remains taut, yet rounded, and their back remains flat. The legs begin to appear shorter and no longer out of proportion. Antlers can be large, as they have attained 90% of their size. The tarsal glands become noticeably larger and darker, chocolate to black. Behaviorally, four-year-olds are the most aggressive and active age class during the rut.

Five-year-olds begin to demonstrate a slight sag in the stomach and a slight drop in the back. Their nose can be rounded and legs appear much thicker.

5½-year-old bucks

At this age bucks are approaching their maximum antler-growing years, thus antlers can be large yet indistinguishable from genetically superior four-year-old males. The principal characteristic defining this age class is an obvious sag in the stomach and a slight drop in the back. The nose is often rounded, losing the square confirmation characteristic of younger males. Their legs appear thicker as well. During the rut their necks are extremely

A much-rounded nose, large belly, and a sagging back with no distinction between the neck and body cavity during the rut are distinguishing characteristics of a six-year-old buck. They also appear to have a larger rump and sad or semi closed eyes. Skin under the chin begins to sag at this age.

Body size is not characteristic of this bruiser of six years because it showed up late in the postrut period after losing an excessive amount of weight. The truth is a hunter shouldn't worry about aging this buck because he is an obvious shooter.

muscled, inflated-like in appearance, eliminating the juncture between the chest and neck. The neck and brisket area appears to become one. Five-year-olds are in peak muscular condition with little sign of aging. The tarsals on some become obviously chocolate brown to wet-black, oftentimes extending down the entire inside of their legs. One other characteristic. Often at this age bucks will start to develop narrow, squinty eyes. Watch for it.

6½-year-old bucks

Lucky is the hunter privileged to see a buck that has reached what is referred to as its golden antler producing year. At six, their physical appearance is similar to five-year-olds; however, one distinguishing feature to look for is obvious loose skin protruding from under the lower jaw. The nose is rounded and the ears no longer terminate to a sharp point. A prominent rounded belly and a sagging back also become obvious. Although deer develop their largest antlers at six years of age in South Texas, it doesn't mean that all six-year-olds will exhibit extremely large antlers because of variable factors such as weather conditions (rainfall) and the animal's genetic potential, which ultimately determine antler size.

7½-year-old bucks

These over mature bucks are extremely rare and sometimes confused for younger deer because their muscular features begin to regress. Loose skin around the face and neck is obvious. Ears are completely rounded at the terminal end with old, healed-over scars sometimes evident. As these animals

Seven-plus-year-old bucks begin to exhibit some regression in body size, particularly during drought. Old healed-over scars, torn ears, and the increased amount of loose skin, particularly under the chin, are features to look for in these monarchs.

Bucks seven years old and older are sometimes confused with younger deer because of weight loss, but they can still produce a substantial set of headgear under ideal climatic conditions.

reduce their breeding activities, recent battle scars are not present but old healed-over scars are evident. Although antler size generally decreases in the over mature age classes, I have witnessed exceptional antler growth in older bucks experiencing ideal range conditions. Matter of fact, I harvested an 8½-year-old (based on tooth wear) buck in 1993 that gross scored 184 and netted 171⅜ inches. Thus antler size alone cannot always be employed to estimate a deer's age. Behaviorally these deer are extremely reticent and often go unobserved until peak-rutting activity is over.

Fawns

I placed fawns last, but in reality mistakes are frequently made on these youngsters. Classifying a deer as a fawn is not difficult; however, distinguishing whether it's a male or female can be challenging. One of the principle tenets of deer management is to balance the sex ratio. Since deer are born evenly distributed between males and females, a ratio of 1:1 is considered more natural.

The accomplishment of this scenario usually requires a substantial doe harvest that often includes fawns. Even when fawns are considered off limits to hunters, they will still show up in the harvest, and a buck removed as a fawn is a mistake. Some fawns, particularly males, late in the hunting season can develop an above-average body size and be difficult to distinguish from young adult doe. So, let's start here and talk about telling the difference between does and fawns.

One key characteristic is body size and shape

An adult doe is more rectangular, while the fawn looks square. The head of a doe is long and slender while the fawn's head is short and compact. Behavior is also helpful. A fawn is less wary than an adult doe. Fawns are also more submissive, more playful, and more inquisitive than an adult doe.

Now let's consider how to tell buck fawns from doe fawns. Obviously, the presence of buttons is a major clue to a buck. Hunters must employ a quality optic, but even then the hair-covered antler pedicels on these larger fawns are difficult to see. Buck fawns have flatter, less-rounded heads, larger bodies (except in late fall), and are more aggressive and inquisitive than doe fawns. A buck fawn is extremely curious and normally will remain in sight much longer than the females. My theory here is if it doesn't run off, don't shoot it.

One other behavioral trait; button bucks are more likely to be traveling alone in the hunting season than doe fawns.

Much of the information I reviewed is the result of years observing, studying, and hunting deer. Employing a unique capture technique and critiquing a variety of body and antler characteristics from 766 free-ranging bucks, Dr. Mickey Hellickson researched this subject over a 13-year period to determine if certain features could significantly improve one's ability to age bucks on the hoof.

Statistical results of Hellickson's research indicated that antler gross score was the best antler characteristic for estimating age proceeded by basal circumference and inside spread of antlers.

The best body characteristic for estimating age was stomach girth. However, none of the body characteristics were significantly different for bucks 2½ years of age or older. Combining characteristics, the two that work best for aging live deer are gross Boone and Crockett score and stomach girth. Based on Hellickson's research, chest girth increases with age as does the gross Boone and Crockett score. However, estimating chest girth is extremely difficult in the field. It really presents a challenge when time is limited.

The most efficient method of estimating a buck's age on the hoof is to become familiar with antler measurements after the buck is harvested. Since physical characteristics collected as harvest data can be employed to estimate a live buck's age, sportsmen should become knowledgeable with antler and body sizes for each age class of bucks taken on their hunting lands. This can only be done by collecting and reviewing harvest data. If none exist, begin collecting this valuable information. It not only addresses management decisions and progress, but it facilitates one's ability to age and score deer in the field. By acquiring this information, you will also become more familiar with the scoring process as well. Thus when a particular buck appears during the hunting season, you will be able to age him with more confidence and precision.

Estimating a deer's age on the hoof is no less challenging than first locating the animal. With experience, it can be accomplished but mistakes are inevitable. Antler size and body condition remain dependent on the nutritional components of the habitat and this can be as variable as the weather that dictates the quality and abundance of forage required by deer.

Accomplished deer hunters are adept at estimating the Boone and Crockett score of deer, but when it comes to aging a deer on the hoof, even the experts have trouble on occasion. The fact is that estimating the age of live deer is nothing more than an educated guess that improves with experience. The more deer one has seen, the better they become at estimating their age—after all, that's all it is—an estimate.

Hunter: *I don't understand why aging a buck is so important. I hunt in areas where there are few older bucks, so whether the buck I harvest is 2½, 3½, or 4½ makes little difference. Why bother?*

Bob/Dave: *At one time, for almost all hunters, being able to age bucks on the hoof was of little consequence. Then along came quality deer management, where individuals were trying to maximize the quality of the does and bucks on their land. With habitat and harvest management, hunters on such properties started seeing bigger bucks, and then came a need to be able to age bucks on the hoof to maximize their growth before harvest. Whether you age bucks on the hoof so as to restrict your harvest is up to you. It is an individual or a property owner's choice.*

Hunter: *I read that one should wait on a 4½ or 5½-year-old buck or older rather than shoot a younger one. What is that all about?*

Bob/Dave: *I covered a bit of this in the previous question, but the 4½-5½-year-old category is one that some landowners utilize because it is at that age, that bucks reach their maximum. Thus, they chose to let their bucks reach that age before any bucks are harvested. For many hunters, such a choice doesn't exist simply because there are few older bucks where they hunt. But, where the management practices are aimed at quality deer management, passing up younger bucks, harvesting lots of does, and passing up button bucks, then you may reach a point where you can restrict all buck harvest to those that are fully mature.*

Deer rely heavily on their olfactory system (sense of smell). They not only use smell to identify danger, but also to locate and follow estrus does.

CHAPTER 5

Reading a Deer's Body Language

The only thing that prevented deer feeding in the grain field from seeing me was a hog plum bush. It was the first week of December in South Texas. The rut was about to start, and I expected to see several bucks in search of receptive does.

As the sun dipped below the tree line, a mature eight-pointer entered the field, and immediately began to feed. Moments later, his head sprang up and with ears slanted forward; he stared towards the edge of the field. Two does with fawns appeared and as the fawns dashed onto the field, the buck flicked its tail and continued feeding, lifting his head only when he had a mouthful of grain. The tail flick has several meanings. It occurs when deer feed and there is no reason for alarm. They also do it when slightly disturbed, right before they walk away.

Moments later, the buck whipped his head upright, laid his ears back, and stared into the thorny brush. His tan coat darkened as the hair on the animal's back and flank bristled erect. I knew he had just detected another buck, as this was aggressive behavior. Suddenly a doe appeared from behind a small persimmon motte and I heard several low, guttural grunts behind her. I strained to see through the tangled branches when a buck appeared. I counted 12 tines decorated with several atypical points on the 22-inch-wide rack, but the deer failed to remain visible long enough for me to estimate its score. With head down, he dashed back and forth, much like a cutting horse, attempting to haze the doe into a vulnerable position.

As light faded, I realized I wasn't going to get a shot, so I crawled away without disturbing the deer.

Two mornings later, I entered a cramped, elevated box blind located near the motte the doe used to evade the large buck two days earlier. Shortly after I stepped into the blind, two fawns entered the field. Extending my rattling antlers outside the blind, I ground the appendages together lightly for approximately 40 seconds.

Almost immediately, a doe appeared, heading to the field. I noticed that her tail was semi erect. This told me that she was about to come into estrus. There had to be a buck close by. As she entered the field, she showed no interest in feeding and simply stared into the brush with ears erect. Had she been looking at me, I would not have moved, because she was on alert. But she stared into the brush so I knew a deer had to be in there. Thus, I had my rifle in position when the buck first appeared, but couldn't see antlers because, like a bird dog working a covey of quail, his head was low and constantly moving. He stared at the doe after entering the grain field, not 30 yards away. Finally I had the opening and saw that he was the super buck. With one shot the 184-inch, 17-point collapsed and the brush country provided me another precious memory.

Taking this buck was not all luck. I capitalized on hard-earned knowledge of deer behavior. First, I avoided detection by lying outside the field until locating a desirable buck. More importantly, I have found that once a particular buck is observed hazing a doe, one has three days to see the deer again before it ventures off after another doe. This three-day window of opportunity is based on the proven theory that bucks will pursue a doe 24 hours before it enters estrus, breed them throughout the 24-hour receptive period, then hang around another day hazing the unreceptive animal. I have employed this strategy often and have taken several outstanding whitetails as a result.

Deer communicate by sight, sound, and smell and employ these senses to detect danger and alert others. When a potential threat is detected, all their senses focus on that object. They give out vocal and visual signals and your most successful hunters have learned to read that deer language. Acquiring this skill takes time. The more deer one observes, the more they learn how deer communicate and respond to various stimuli. There is no question that learning those signals will increase your success.

Ear position

Ear position dictates what a deer is thinking. When a potential threat is detected, they assume a stereotypic alert posture. With ears cocked forward and with erect hair along their back, they attempt to force the object of concern to move in order to confirm danger. At times they appear to look

With ears laid forward, deer alertly scan the brush for potential danger.

away when they are actually using their eyesight in a more efficient manner.

A deer's principal alarm signal is the snort. A raised tail precedes this vocalization while the animal drives one of its front hooves firmly into the ground. Does snort at many objects and are often ignored by other deer, unless the target of concern (for example, a hunter) moves, or wind delivers the hunter's scent to the animal

One efficient method of viewing a large number of deer is to sneak up on food plots. I frequently sneak up to these deer magnets, but sometimes get busted. The alarmed deer, usually a doe, will raise her tail, drive a foot continually into the ground, even bound off a few feet only to whirl around and repeat this behavior all over again. I simply lay flat on the ground and relax while she carries on. The more she fusses, the less attention other deer in the field direct towards her, and before long she will return to feeding, allowing me to reach a desirable observation point.

An alarmed deer will drive their front feet into the ground to elicit a response by the object it is focused upon. A common occurrence with doe but once a buck drives its foot into the ground a couple times, it is gone.

The white underside of a deer's tail, exposed in the erect position, is accepted by all deer as the ultimate warning of pending danger.

Bucks react differently

A buck fawn is curious and may approach an unidentified object. A mature buck that snorts may drive its foot into the ground a couple of times, but they then depart immediately. Old bucks leave little to chance; that's why they get old. When a deer is relatively close to you and snorts, bobs his/her head and stomps his/her front feet, you probably only have a few seconds to shoot before the deer takes off. If you are bowhunting and the deer is out of range, you might try a fawn bleat (on a doe) or a grunt-snort-wheeze call (see Chapter 6) to calm them down and draw them closer for a shot.

*With ears laid back and hair on their neck erect, these two mature monarchs
are focused on one thing, each other. That's a great time for a hunter
to move closer for a shot.*

When a deer raises its upper lip, it's not to decipher whether an object is dangerous or not, but to distinguish whether a doe is in estrus.

Deer rely most on their olfactory system (sense of smell). A doe may snort, and drive its feet into the ground to elicit a response, but if she detects human scent, she disappears.

Another behavior to watch for is the stiff legged walk. Deer will do this when they feel something is wrong, but they haven't quite pinned down the problem.

A knowledge of body language is especially useful during the rut (breeding season). As an example, on the hunt described at the beginning of this chapter, I knew immediately that the first deer approaching was a doe by the behavior exhibited by the buck. Whenever a potential threat is detected, adult bucks exhibit an alert posture characterized by ears cocked forward and erect hair along their backs. If the object remains motionless, foot stomping is a deer's attempt to force the object to move.

Competition between deer is not solely over position in the breeding hierarchy, but throughout the year for cover and food.

If the threat is identified as dangerous, the tail will spring upward, providing a clue to other deer that there is potential danger. Following the erect tail response, the hair on the rump and tail will flair up, representing an immediate cue to dash off. A doe fleeing danger will wag her erect tail back and forth, exposing the ostentatious white underside coercing observers to flee as well.

Young bucks, particularly yearlings, frequently spar. Over time, they assume a social rank based on strength. At age two and older, mature bucks sometimes move from sparring to fighting. When so doing his intimidation posture is different. When a male competitor is observed, ears are laid back, and his sleek coat bristles up making him appear dark in color.

Three to four-year-old bucks are the most aggressive animals in a deer herd continually competing for a position in the breeding hierarchy. They frequently clash with other bucks, but in a healthy herd with even older, more mature bucks, their breeding privileges are reduced. These older boys do the majority (but not all) of the breeding. (We cover more on who does the breeding in chapter 10).

Aggression between males intensifies during the rut. A number of bucks can feed together during the rut with only an occasional display of aggression, but the appearance of a new buck is quite dramatic. When two five or six-year-old bucks meet during the breeding season, it is a dramatic event. With ears laid back, the hair on their backs and along their sides bristles up exhibiting a chameleon-like change in color from tan to almost black. They will sidle up to each other; walk side by side as if to size each other up before their antlers come together. You can often hear the grunt-snort-wheeze call right before they clash antlers. This initial contact can be rather quiet, or it might be a loud crash. Regardless of the initial impact, once

Deer bond throughout the antler-growing period
employing pheromones (odors) to identify cohorts.

the antlers touch, things quickly erupt into one horrendous pushing match.

Combat can last a few seconds to several minutes. The longest fight I ever witnessed, endured for eight minutes. Basically, the fight continues until one of the combatants stumbles or falls. Once this occurs, the subordinate animal normally dashes off, but not always. In many cases they reunite in one loud clash of antlers and the battle continues until one turns tail.

Injuries in such fights do occur. Eyes can be damaged, and antler punctures and cuts can occur. It is not common, but during these confrontations, injuries can be fatal. At times antlers will become entwined, insuring the demise of both gladiators.

Though fighting is most common during the rut, it is not isolated to that time as deer establish dominance throughout the year. In the summer deer compete for forage, cover, and water. In these altercations, deer rise up on their hind legs and flail away at their opponent with their front feet.

The predictable fashion with which deer respond to various stimuli affords hunters valuable seconds to prepare for a shot. For example, if a buck suddenly focuses its attention on a particular location, a hunter should focus on that same point. If the animal's ears retract, or you hear a grunt-snort-wheeze call, or their hair coat bristles up changing to a darker color, it's apparent another buck is nearby.

Another important cue is the tail flick. A deer will wag its tail before moving off. Spooked deer perform this same activity once they calm down. The tail flick is a universal signal that everything is all right.

Knowledge of deer behavior is acquired by observing deer. No text can replace experience, and nothing forces a hunter to learn more about it than blowing a golden opportunity on a trophy buck simply because they misread the animal's body language.

Hunter: *This material is interesting, but I'm not sure how it helps me have more success. What's the big deal here?*

Bob/Dave: *In many hunting situations you need to know what the deer is going to do next. For example, let's say you have a doe and a big buck feeding in front of you, moving toward you slowly, but still out of range. The doe is off to your left around 100 yards from the buck. The buck is now in range of you, but not standing in a position where you can take the shot. This is the most critical moment for you today. In fact, this might be the most critical moment for you for the whole year. The buck begins to flick his tail, telling you that he may start walking away. You are seriously thinking of taking the shot, even though the distance is a bit far. Then a second doe enters the field only twenty yards from your stand, and her tail is erect. This tells you that she is probably in estrus, and it tells that buck the same thing. Now you know you can wait for a better shot, for almost certainly that buck is going to move toward this second doe.*

    Every time you observe deer they are giving signals to each other, and to you. Your job is to understand what they are saying to each other and use that to your advantage.

Hunter: *Obviously behavior around the stand is most important. My question relates to hunting bucks from a tree stand. Is it better to have a doe around the stand or scare them away so that they don't scent you and give an alarm when a buck comes into the area?*

Bob/Dave: *You always want other deer, especially does, around when hunting bucks, because they act as living decoys. If a doe is feeding undisturbed near you that sends a positive signal to any deer that everything is fine in that area. Of course, if you're in pre-rut or rut, all the better as a doe is exactly what bucks are looking for. Yes, a doe could scent you at the wrong time and take the buck away with her, but it is definitely worth the gamble. Does near you are a good thing.*

Like all techniques, talking to deer does not always work, but when it works, another element of excitement and accomplishment is afforded to serious deer hunters.

CHAPTER 6

Calling All Deer, Come In Please

I n 1978, while driving to deer hunt in Canaan Valley, my (DS) good friend Len Cardinale taught me to call deer. It wasn't high-powered science, just a grunting noise with the mouth. "Urp." The rules were simple, and they still work today. If you see a buck and he is not going to come your way, grunt at him. If the buck starts your way, do not call. If he turns to leave, call.

Len told me that grunting at deer would not scare deer. "They may not always respond, but you will rarely scare them. You have nothing to lose, so call," Len said. Three hours later, a dandy eight pointer was walking 100 yards from my stand, so I grunted. He walked closer, and then turned, so I called again. He walked closer, and then started the other direction, so I called, and this time he came. I shot under him at thirty yards, but it was very windy, so the buck didn't really know what happened. He did run, but then walked away. At sixty yards, I called again, and back he came. This time I didn't miss.

Like rattling, grunting up deer has been around for a long time, becoming popular to the hunting public in the late 1970s.

That was the first buck I've talked to, but I've had discussions with hundreds since that time. I now call almost every time I hunt. I've expanded my repertoire, and now use other calls. For example, I often use the Primos Can doe-in-estrus call to bring in bucks. I also have added the buck-snort-wheeze call in certain situations and the growl as well. Sometimes the calls work, sometimes they don't. It's hard to know what is going on in a deer's psyche that determines whether they will come when you call. Take the doe-in-estrus "Can" call. Two years ago in November, in Alberta, a dandy ten point walked behind my stand. At sixty yards I called. Nothing. He just stood there. The wind was in my favor, when I called a second time. This time he took off the other way like he'd been shot with a gun. I have no idea why he reacted that way. They usually do nothing, and once in awhile, they will come in. This guy ran. Go figure.

The next morning my buddy was in a stand three hundred yards from that location. That same ten pointer (he ended up weighing in at 308 pounds, so he was one of those Alberta bruisers) got into a nasty fight with

When a buck is walking away, hunters have nothing to lose by calling to the animal. Sometimes they do not respond immediately, but circle back later to investigate.

a larger buck (yes, this second buck weighed more than 308 pounds). They smashed trees, tore up the brush, and after three minutes or so, the smaller buck lost the fight. The winner walked straight away, across an alfalfa field. A few minutes later my friend used the Can call and the loser in the fight came right to him and that was it. The shot was true, and we weighed him later that day. Why did he run from that call the day before? I'll never know. But he responded to my friend's calling even though he'd lost the fight. Maybe his psyche said, "OK, I hear a doe in estrus calling, and the dominant buck has left the area, so I'll just go up there and introduce myself."

Bob Zaiglin attracts many mature bucks in by combining his rattling technique with continuous guttural grunts.

Back to the grunt call

Don't expect too much when using this call. In my experience, when you see a buck and grunt at him, he may look your way, but most of the time he just keeps on doing whatever he was doing. He may drift your way slowly, and that's good, but do not expect to grunt at a deer and have him charge in. It just doesn't happen very often.

In the rut, things change, and the grunt call definitely brings in bucks. Not always, but nothing works all the time. When he gets in range, but you don't have a shot, try a grunt call. It often gives you that few extra steps you need.

I've often heard stories from bowhunters where, if they had used a grunt call with the mouth, a bow shot might have occurred. For example, the deer is walking and won't stop for a shot. At full draw, just use your mouth and grunt at him. You see them do it on TV all the time, and it works. How about when a deer is just ten yards out of range and headed away? Just grunt at him. Use your mouth and grunt. You don't have time to fool with a store-bought call. Go ahead and grunt, you have nothing to lose.

What if you don't have your bow or gun ready for the shot and the buck is walking away? Grunt at him while grabbing your bow or gun. What do you have to lose? Consider this all-to-common situation. You are stalking a buck, and are almost in range when you stumble in the leaves, or kick a limb, or do something to make noise that should alert the buck. Grunt softly and he just might continue feeding. He hears grunts all the time. Grunts are not alarm calls to a deer. They are calls he hears every day, especially in the fall.

Bottom line; do not be afraid to grunt. If the deer is walking a long way off, grunt loud so he will hear the call. He may not look at you, but you can usually tell by his body language that he heard the call. Once, in Michigan, a buck was following a doe around 100 yards from my stand. I grunted loudly and I knew he heard it, but he kept following that doe out of sight. Twenty minutes later, there he was, coming back by himself. I grunted

As quality deer management became popular, an increase in mature bucks equating to increased competition between males augmented the effectiveness of the grunt call.

again and he walked to me and right into my freezer. Hmmm, maybe there is something to calling deer.

Remember when the rattling craze started?

It was back in the early 1980's and to listen to some of the speakers who touted rattling, one got the impression that it would draw in big bucks every time. Back then folks in Texas were the rattlers. It took some convincing to get those of us in other states to even give it a try. And when it didn't work for us, we quit doing it. *For the latest on rattling, see Chapter 7.*

Every year the innovative hunting industry comes out with new products for hunters. Most are simply spin-offs of something old that the industry just repackages with more glamour. However, there are two deer calls out that I think have great potential for increasing your hunting success and enjoyment. Both may bring in mature bucks, and with the extra push on improving the number of mature bucks out there, these calls can really be used to your advantage.

The first call is the "grunt-snort-wheeze," and my good friend Barry Wensel first brought my attention to the value of using this call. The grunt-snort-wheeze call is given in very aggressive situations when one buck encounters another, when a hot doe is nearby. This is a great call to use when you see a mature buck or when you think one is in the area. I also use it during the chase phase of the rut, to blind call occasionally from my tree stand. Why not? You have nothing to lose. Last year I even was able to bring in a decent Illinois 8 pointer that was chasing a hot doe. M.A.D. Game Calls (www.madgamecalls.com) makes a grunt-snort-wheeze call, but you can easily do this call with your mouth. In fact I'd rather just use my mouth because it is easier and quicker than pulling out a call. Simply place your top front teeth on the inside of your lower gum and loudly blow out three quick and short times. "Phhht, phhht, phhht." Then finish with one loud and long, extended "phhhhhhhhhhhhhhhhht" call, blowing thru your upper front teeth. It won't scare deer (few attempted deer calls do) and it can work.

The second call is new. Actually I don't think there is anything new about this call. I think it is just an extended, louder, more emotional, aggressive version of the tending grunt call. Right now two companies are selling this new call, Mad Game Calls and Primos Hunting Calls. I think they are really onto something with this call, but time will tell. M.A.D. calls its the Buck Growl call, while Promos calls its the Buck Roar call. Either way I think the whole concept is interesting. I can't make this call with my mouth so I will be using the manufactured versions this fall.

Prior to last summer, I'd never heard about this call. Growing up in Pennsylvania before the days of antler restrictions and living in West Virginia where most bucks get hammered as yearlings, I haven't been exposed to many mature bucks. And it is the mature bucks that give and respond to this call.

After looking at the promotional video put out by Mad Game Calls, I'm convinced that in some situations, this call can work. Use this call in late October and early November when bucks are chasing does. Bucks exhibiting a high level of emotion in the rut give the growl call. They give it when trying to get an estrus doe to stop, or as a warning to other bucks to leave the doe alone. A hot doe is always involved. You can also hear it when bucks get ready to fight. It is simply a high-level aggressive call given by a buck to announce that he is after, or on, a hot doe and you should leave her alone. She is mine. Get out.

Why would a buck respond to that? Simply because it usually means a hot doe is nearby. The responding buck will come in to check it out. If he is more dominant than the buck already there (in this case, it is you), then he will challenge that buck and take over the doe if possible.

To use the call, you start by giving the short, normal tending grunt call. Grunt rather quietly several times, then make the grunt call longer and much louder, which gives the "growl" or "roar."

Use this call to bring in bucks to what they think is a buck chasing a hot doe. One of M.A.D.'s video scenes shows a buck harassing a doe. The buck gives this call repeatedly, especially when other bucks start coming into the area. You can also use this call while rattling. These calls are not a panacea. And I'd be a bit careful when using them. You don't want to over do them and end up ruining a situation where a big buck is using an area and you screw it up for good. But, if you are confident, then go for it.

Fawns communicate by vocalizations and locate their dams by scent.

Hunter: *OK Dave, I believe you. You can call deer, and apparently hunters should not be afraid to try because it will work every time. Right?*

Dave/Bob: *Well, not every time. But my point is that deer are vocal, and their calls have meaning. If we learn what those meanings are, we can increase our chances of success when calling deer.*

Hunter: *What is the worst mistake I can make when trying to call deer with any call?*

Dave/Bob: *That's an easy one to answer. Two things will do you in when calling deer. Calling too loud, but an even bigger problem is calling too often. Here is a great rule of thumb when calling deer. If the buck is coming your way, do not call at all. If he hangs up, then you might lightly tickle horns together or lightly grunt at him. Or you might Can call him. Movement at this time can also do you in, so any movements must be slow and quiet.*

Hunter: *So, calling doesn't work every time, but why not?*

Dave/Bob: *Sometimes the deer can't hear your calls. A soft grunt call may not reach that buck; so crank it up a notch so that he can hear it. Another reason calling doesn't always work is because we don't know the mental state of the deer. They've got to be in the right mood. Let's say that you give the tending grunt call to a buck you've spotted from your tree stand. Three grunt calls given with a pause in between. Now, a buck following a doe in heat gives this call and that is why bucks respond. They come thinking there is a doe in heat there. However, if the buck you are trying to call had a negative encounter with a bigger buck the day before, a bigger buck that was following a doe in heat, then your buck may not come in. He came to that call the day before and got whipped by a big buck. Thus, he may be a bit hesitant to run in to a tending grunt call. There is one other* point to make here. Certain times of the deer season are better calling times than others. In my experience the 2-3 weeks prior to the peak of the rut are the very best times to call deer. The week after peak breeding isn't a bad time either. And weather might make some times better for calling. If a cold front is coming, I call often. Bucks are moving around and thus, may respond to your calls.

Hunter: *I see the problem, so now what do I do?*

Dave/Bob: *Don't expect success every time you call, and be creative. Try the tending grunt call. And as described above, try the aggressive grunt-snort-wheeze- call or the growl call when you see a big buck out there. And, if you need to stop a buck for a bow or gun shot, then use your mouth to grunt at him.*

Hunter: *I've been in such situations and I don't want to frighten off deer by making a poor call.*

Dave/Bob: *This is the major reason hunters do not call. The truth is that you will rarely frighten deer when you call, regardless of how bad your imitation is. When you try calling to deer, you gain confidence and then are not as afraid to call in the future. Remember, the key isn't to call a lot; the key is to assess each situation and call when it can help. Call when your options are dwindling. Watch the wind, because deer coming to calls will circle downwind. You may want to use barriers that prevent deer from moving downwind of your stand when you call. Set up on a shore of a lake, a steep bank, or impenetrable cover, or a fence, or whatever might deter a buck from coming in downwind. In other words, tweak the location you are calling from if possible. A decoy upwind of your position might help too. Calling isn't a magic pill, but you can use deer calls to your advantage in some instances. Give it a try.*

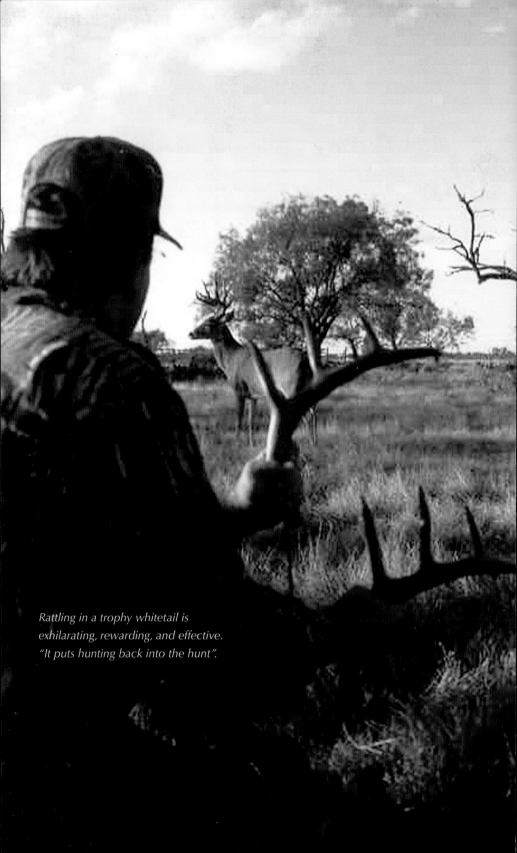

*Rattling in a trophy whitetail is
exhilarating, rewarding, and effective.
"It puts hunting back into the hunt".*

CHAPTER 7

Rattle
Their Cage

S itting beneath a lime-green huisache tree, I (RZ) prepared to perform
my best imitation of a knockdown, drag-out fight between two mature
South Texas bucks. Concealed by the evergreen's drooping branches,
I made several low-pitched guttural grunts before pounding the tips of my
rattling antlers into the ground for almost a minute. Pausing momentarily,
I scanned the openings in the thick chaparral for movement. After a five-
minute break, I began to tear down some of the tree's winter-killed branches
with my hands, making as much racket as possible. I snapped the dry, brittle
wood while clashing and rubbing the antlers. When I finally looked up from
my work, a tremendous buck stood nearby.

The dark-caped buck stood less than 20 steps away, intensely focused
in my direction. When I stopped tearing at the fallen limbs and made eye
contact with the buck, it whirled around and disappeared into the brush. I
resumed clashing the antlers and raking the brush, and the buck returned for
a final, curious look. Taking careful aim, I squeezed the trigger, dropping the
wide-racked, tall-tined 10-pointer.

Most hunters have tried to rattle bucks, and their results have been mixed. Many quit after trying a few times with no success, but I believe that with the following knowledge, rattling can work for you. Experiences like I just described show that rattling is one of the most exciting ways to pursue whitetails. Unlike many hunting methods, rattling lets the hunter take an active role in the pursuit, and more importantly, it can be productive for almost anyone.

Today, rattling has become an inseparable part of the deer hunter's regimen of buck-busting tools. It is exciting, easy and effective. However, to realize its full potential, you must understand the technique and why deer respond to it.

First, the sounds of deer fighting are common in the wild. Throughout the year, deer spar to establish the social hierarchy of the herd. Even does commonly fight by standing erect on their hind legs and "boxing" their

Bucks are not alone when it comes to fighting as all deer compete for food, water, and cover. Does use their sharp hooves to declare dominance.

competitors into submission with their front hoofs. Bucks engage in this way, too, but in late fall and winter, they cease such behavior and use their antlers for fighting. This is the best time to rattle.

The principal component of rattling is antlers. Synthetic and real antlers work equally well. I use sheds from two right beams. The beams are medium weight and have three 7-inch tines. I don't use a matched set because when I slam non-matched antlers together, the points move away from each other, reducing the chance of injuring my hands. I have removed the brow tines, rounded the tips and sanded the bases to reduce the chance of puncturing my hands and increase comfort. Rough bases not only wear out gloves, they are also uncomfortable to use. Although I prefer these antlers for comfort reasons, *any antlers will attract deer*. The size and shape of rattling antlers is up to the individual.

As most hunters know, rattling mimics the sounds of a fight between two bucks competing for breeding privileges. When an aggressive buck searching for a receptive doe hears a fight, it might lock in on the location and check it out, not necessarily to fight, but more importantly to intercept the doe the bucks are fighting over.

Rattling methods are as diverse as the personalities of hunters

The best technique is the one that your experience has shown most effective and at the end of this chapter we present scientific data that will help you chose a rattling technique. The key is to be confident. Rattling works so don't be afraid to investigate ways to improve your technique.

Although I usually use my preferred rattling procedure, I adjust my base technique to match each situation. My basic technique begins as I drive the tips of the beams alternately into the ground for about a minute, imitating the sound of a buck's hoofs as it chases a doe. After a brief pause, I aggressively rub the back of the beams together, then reverse the antlers and tick the tines lightly. I do this for about a minute.

After another brief pause, while continually scanning for movement, I clash and grind the antlers together, loudly at first, then lightly toward the end of a 1½ minute sequence. I then pause several minutes and repeat this last sequence every five to 10 minutes.

I usually stay at rattling sites 15 to 25 minutes, and then change locations. However, if I've seen a particularly large buck in the area, I sometimes hunt that location several hours, rattling every 30 to 40 minutes. Although rattling usually elicits a response from deer, distance or the animal's temperament might prolong a deer's approach.

To estimate rattling's success rate and response time, I kept a detailed log describing 145 rattling sequences I made in 1989. Forty-five of the 145 attempts called in at least one buck - a success rate of 31 percent. The elapsed time between the rattling and a confirmed response ranged from 30 seconds to 30 minutes. Some bucks charged in before I had a chance to set the antlers down, while others were hesitant and required coaxing before

A balanced sex ratio is not only more natural, it increases competition amongst bucks for breeding privileges, augmenting the effectiveness of the rattling technique.

they appeared. The average response time was five minutes. Because of varied responses, you must be prepared for surprises while rattling. If not, you might miss the opportunity of a lifetime.

Renowned outdoor writer Gary Clancy notes that there are four factors that help to determine success or failure from rattling. First, the buck to doe ratio must be good. Having relatively equal numbers of adult, mature, bucks and does means there is more competition for does. The more competition, the better mature bucks respond to rattling. It's important to note that the ranch where I conducted my rattling experiment had a 2-to-1 adult doe-to-antlered buck ratio. The adult doe-to-antlered buck ratio is the most decisive factor that affects rattling's effectiveness because competition between bucks for breeding privileges is highest in herds with a balanced sex ratio. However, even in deer herds with overabundant does, rattling is sometimes successful. That's because such herds have pockets with balanced sex ratios. Locating these places is the key to effective rattling.

Clancy's second factor is time of the year, and I'll give you the latest scientific data on this in a minute. Hunting pressure can also be a factor. If there are a lot of gun hunters in the woods, getting bucks to respond will obviously be tougher.

Clancy also advises you to have realistic expectations. It doesn't always work like you see on television or videos. The study we report on later in this chapter shows high response rates to rattling. You probably won't get such high response, but what this study does show is that *rattling works a whole lot more than you think it does*. Another factor that affects rattling success is the onset of breeding. The ratio of receptive does per buck narrows substantially after does begin cycling through estrus, forcing bucks to compete more for fewer does and enhancing rattling.

Locating an ideal rattling position is crucial to success regardless of where you hunt. The first things I look for are rubs, tracks and, most importantly, fresh scrapes. If an area has fresh scrapes, a buck is probably nearby.

Tearing away at nearby brush with the antlers simulates the sound of deer fighting enhancing the technique's effectiveness.

An ideal way to see more bucks that are attracted to a mock battle is to employ the buddy system, particularly with one individual situated upwind of the rattler in a tripod, which affords excellent visibility.

Set up in prime areas facing into the wind, because bucks generally circle downwind before approaching. I like to conceal myself without losing the critical downwind view. Since bucks often circle to get down wind of the rattler, consider how to set up so that bucks are restricted when they try to do this. For example, if there is a river or pond that will prevent the buck from circling you, set up there. Or you might set up near an open field where the buck will have to expose himself when he tries to get down wind. Of course, the best solution to this problem is to have a partner who sets up 50 or so yards behind you and does the rattling.

A serious buck confrontation is not a silent affair. When two mature, love-ridden bucks battle, it involves a lot of brush cracking and tree limbs snapping - noises that echo long distances. Because of this noise overload, the sound of clashing antlers is scarcely heard in real buck fights.

The reason young bucks respond most frequently is because they are more prevalent and aggressively attempting to enter the breeding hierarchy of the deer herd.

For example, several years ago, I observed an amazing buck confrontation on a ridge about a half-mile away. During the 10-minute battle, I heard antlers clash only twice. However, the sounds of the bucks crashing through the brush resonated throughout the area during the entire fight. Despite the lack of antler sounds, the fight attracted bucks from every direction. As shown by this encounter, successful rattling involves the other sounds associated with buck fights. To recreate this in my rattling sessions, I conceal my position well, so I can tear up brush without being seen.

While rattling in South Texas, I prefer to set up under mature, umbrella-shaped huarache trees. At a distance, these trees look like giant green mushrooms. Aside from offering a well-concealed calling site, huaraches drop much litter in the way of dead leaves and brittle branches, which I use to augment my rattling. By smashing and cracking old drooping limbs, I further convince bucks that a real fight is taking place.

Rattling in a mature trophy buck is a result of perseverance. Luck is required, but the harder you work, the luckier one gets. The author Bob Zaiglin rattled in this buck right after a weak rain shower in South Texas.

Bucks might approach rattling from any direction, or pause just out of sight. However, they usually come in from downwind, where their noses can warn them of danger. When bucks do this, your chances of seeing them plummet, because bucks smell you before stepping into range. As already mentioned, a good way to trick these wary bucks is to use the buddy system. Station a partner 40 to 50 yards downwind of your rattling setup, preferably in an elevated stand. This will enable your partner to spot weary bucks circling downwind of the calling. When used with three people, this technique is even more effective. The third hunter stands 40 to 50 yards

Rattling is an effective technique to bring in middle-aged bucks during peak rut.
For older monarchs the pre- and post-rut are also great times to rattle.

upwind of the rattler, and often sees more bucks than the other two hunters.

Deceiving a mature buck is not easy no matter where you hunt. However, it is possible. Every year, hunters tell me they have no problem calling in young deer, but they have difficulty fooling mature bucks. I have had the same experiences, but for different reasons than most hunters think. Although young bucks seem easier to rattle in than mature bucks, it's only because they are more common, not more responsive to calling.

Aside from being educated by surviving the gauntlet of at least five or six hunting seasons, big bucks are rare, which decreases the odds of rattling one into range. However, although they aren't pushovers, big bucks will eventually respond to patient, persistent rattling on well-managed lands.

Weather conditions affect deer behavior, including how they respond to rattling. Buck activity surges on cold, cloudy, drizzly days, particularly following prolonged periods of unseasonably warm temperatures. Older bucks seem to drop their guard under these conditions and move more freely. Unfortunately, you can't control the weather. I have rattled in hot conditions— not uncommon in South Texas—and although I wasn't as successful as in cooler temperatures, I still had some luck, particularly during the early morning.

Remember, deer must breed regardless of the temperature or other factors. If negative environmental conditions prevail, you must be flexible and adjust your tactics accordingly. For instance, if deer activity is dramatically reduced because of high temperatures, rattle during the cooler early morning and late afternoon hours. By rattling during the hottest part of the day, you may educate bucks and have low odds of success.

Rattling in a mature buck is a dynamic event.

It doesn't happen all the time, but it can occur any time you head afield. Perseverance is a prerequisite for rattling success, but luck always plays a role. Regardless of your methods, I believe killing a big buck involves a combination of luck and skill. However, the harder you work and the more familiar with techniques like rattling you become, the luckier you get.

For years, there was no reason to look for scientific information on rattling that might give you a better idea of whether it would work or not. There was none. But there is now. Dr. Mickey Hellickson conducted a major rattling study at the Welder Wildlife Foundation Refuge in southern Texas. We won't go into all the details of the study, and there are several parts to that study, but here is the gist of what Mickey did.

Table 1.

Percentage of different age class bucks that responded in the pre-rut, rut, and post-rut.

	Pre-rut*	Rut **	Post-rut***
1½ - 2½	39%	33%	31%
3½ - 4½	28%	48%	34%
5½+	33%	19%	34%

    * In pre-rut 60 rattling sequences attracted 18 bucks (30%)

  ** In peak-rut 60 rattling sequences attracted 65 bucks (107%)

*** In post-rut 51 rattling sequences attracted 29 bucks (57%).

	Time of Day	
7:30-10:30AM	10:30-1:30	1:30-4:30
94%	40%	53%

First, some background on the area. There are telephone pole observation towers placed all over the 8000-acre refuge. The cover is low brush, and it is fairly thick, typical South Texas low brush country. Deer numbers on the refuge are high; the buck-to-doe ratio is fairly balanced, and there are plenty of older mature bucks on the area. There is some hunting on the preserve, but not as much as you find on the areas you hunt. So, one might expect deer here to be less wary, at least a little less wary, than in areas with heavy hunting pressure. Given that, one might expect that the response rate to rattling might also be higher than in most places.

In the first phase of the study, Mickey placed an observer in the tower to watch for bucks while he rattled from the ground. In a second phase of the study, Mickey had activity collars on some older bucks. With these collars he could not only tell if a buck moved, but he could also tell the direction they took.

Mickey wanted to know how successful rattling was, and what type or rattling worked best. So he set up a number of duplications. They rattled loud (where you bang the antlers together), and soft (where you tickle the points, and grind the bases together). They rattled long (7 minutes of rattling followed by 3 minutes of silence) and short (1 minute of rattling and 9 minutes of silence). They combined these two techniques with long-loud, long-soft, short-loud, and short-soft rattling. They rattled in the pre-rut, the rut, and the post-rut. They rattled in all kinds of weather, and at different times of the day. Neat study and here is what they found.

Mickey and his helpers rattled 171 sequences over three years and 111 bucks responded. Whoa. That seems like a lot of bucks and a high response rate. Remember though, these were the bucks seen by the man in the tower, and/or the man on the ground doing the rattling. But here is an interesting bit of data. The guy on the ground only saw 33 % of the bucks that the guy in the tower saw. Why is that?

Well, 66% of the bucks just didn't come far enough for the guy on the ground to see them. They also noted that 67 of the 111 bucks that responded to rattling were first seen down wind. Almost certainly some bucks circled downwind and probably took off before they were seen. Clearly being higher, being off the ground, also gives you a better chance of seeing an approaching buck.

And being able to observe that buck, see him stop, will give you an advantage. When you see him hang up, you may just need to grunt at him, or rattle again, of give the growl or the buck-snort-wheeze call.

What this study shows is that bucks do respond positively to rattling and they respond better than we ever suspected. Now, how do we get all of them to come into bow or gun range? That is the big question. However, Dr. Hellickson does have some answers. For example, he found that loud rattling brings in three times as many bucks as soft rattling. Early morning is best, peak-rut is best, less wind is best, cool temperatures are best, and 75 percent or more cloud cover is best.

Should you rattle short periods (one minute) or long (say 3 minutes at a time)? Remember, the researchers did three 10-minute rattling sequences. *Relative to short or long rattling, they found no difference.* More bucks came during the first rattling sequence, but a good number came during the third sequence, so you need to sit tight for at least 30 minutes when rattling.

As you might surmise, the peak rut was the best time to rattle. Table 1 shows that yearling bucks seem to respond a little better in the pre-rut, but so do the very old bucks. Good, mature 3-½ and 4-½ years-old bucks responded best in the peak of the rut. *The really older bucks seem to respond* less in the peak-rut and *more in the post-rut.* In fact, of the 29 bucks that responded during the post-rut, 10 were in the 3½ and 4½ age category and another 10 were 5½ and older. Obviously, that post-rut is a great time to rattle.

Loud rattling is best, except for the bigger bucks. Big bucks came during the pre and post-rut more so than during the peak-rut. But (and here is the gold nugget of data that rattlers will find important), greater numbers of bigger bucks came to soft rattling during the post-rut. When you are after big bucks, rattle softly in the post-rut. Tickle those antlers softly, and grind the bases together, imitating two bucks pushing and shoving.

Is it better to rattle in the morning or afternoon? *Early morning response rates were by far the highest (Table 1).*

The researchers also went into the field and rattled to bucks that had activity collars on and were bedded. These collars allowed the researchers to know when the bucks moved, and in which direction they moved. Pretty neat. They rattled 33 times to these bucks and 24 came closer. As before, only 33% were seen, but bedded bucks did respond positively to rattling.

The average distance moved was ⅓ of a mile, but several bucks came considerably further. Also note that in some cases it was thirty minutes before the bucks came near the rattler. This study tells us that blind rattling works, but we need to be as scent free as possible so those bucks will come in all the way.

Next question. *Do bucks learn to avoid rattling?*

To answer this, the researchers again went to bucks that were bedded. Dr. Hellickson rattled four different times over a few week period to eleven bucks that were 4½ years old or older. You would think that these old timers would be wise to the ways of rattling. And, indeed, some were. One 9½-year-old buck never moved during any of the rattling sequences.

However, 6 of 11 came twice, and 1 of 11 came all 4 times. Four didn't come the first time, but came the second. So, indeed, even these old bucks responded to rattling and some came more than once during a two-week period.

No, this study doesn't give us all the answers and your hunting area probably doesn't have as many older bucks as they had on the Welder Refuge. But you cannot argue with the results that show that bucks respond to rattling more than we thought. In fact, if you use these results in your rattling this coming season, your odds will definitely go up. There is no question. In the right situation, rattling definitely works.

Hunter: *Wow, I had no idea that rattling could work. I tried it a few years back when hunters started talking about it, but I had no success, and figured it wasn't worth the effort. Apparently I was wrong.*

Bob/Dave: *It is like anything else. It doesn't work all the time, and different parts of the country have differing buck to doe ratios that will affect success rates, but rattling definitely can work.*

Hunter: *This coming in downwind thing could be a problem. Obviously if you have a partner rattling 200 feet behind you, that will help. In that situation the bucks may well get to me before they begin to circle downwind of the rattler. But, if you are alone, is there anything you can do?*

Bob/Dave: *Actually, there may be. Woods Wise Calls (www.woodswise.com) has a new product called the Rattle Trap that is a box with a place to attach a string. Dr. Dave has used it in two ways. He ties his bow line to the trap and drops it to the ground under his stand. Then he pulls on the string and it rattles. Being on the ground allows it to also shake dead leaves making it all the more realistic. One great advantage to this Rattle Trap is the fact that your hands are free to shoot as you rattle. Just tug on the string and it rattles. Very little hand movement, and you don't have to hang the antlers up to get ready when a buck responds. Another way to use it is to run a long string, maybe 200 feet if you wish, behind your tree stand and tie it onto the trap. This means that the rattling is coming from behind you and that buck may just hang up right in front of your stand. Dr. Dave has found that if you can anchor the Rattle Trap to the ground all the better. This book is not about pushing equipment, but this little Rattle Trap is a gem of an idea.*

Of course another trick is to simply tie your rattling horns to your bow or gun line and lower them to the ground and rattle them in the leaves. No question this approach has been successful.

Hunter: *Seems like rattling in the morning is the best time. Does this mean I shouldn't bother in late afternoons?*

Bob/Dave: *Not really, because Dr. Hellickson got good responses in the evening, but by far the best time is early morning*

Hunter: *I'm puzzled now, should I bang the antlers together as loud as possible and bust the brush as well, or should I just tickle the bases together?*

Bob/Dave: *There is no one good answer to this question. Loud rattling works best, but the data show that soft rattling in the post rut is a great way to get the really big bucks to come in. This soft rattling probably works in the post rut because you still have a few does in heat and the smaller bucks may scuffle over a hot doe they have found. When the big guy hears this, he comes in to check it out and claim the doe.*

Hunter: *What about calling when I rattle?*

Bob/Dave: *Do it. Mix in several calls as you rattle. Do some grunt calls, and definitely grunt-snort-wheeze calls. I've even thrown in the "can" call on occasion while rattling. There is a lot going on when two bucks get it on. There are other smaller bucks in the area and usually some does as well. And we know that big bucks talk to each other before and during fights. So calling while rattling is worth doing.*

This 195-inch South Texas monster taken in January, 2004 moved a GPS obtained 2.2 miles each December to reach its core breeding area.

CHAPTER 8

How Home Range
Impacts Hunting

I t's happened to every deer hunter I know. You spend the summer and
early fall scouting for deer, and spot several dandy bucks feeding in a
local alfalfa field right before dark. In fact, there are several really good
bucks and a couple of smaller ones traveling together. Well, you assume
they are traveling together because they are always feeding together.

Two of the bucks you recognize from last fall when they were 2½ year
olds. Good bucks, but you passed one of them up with your bow because
you knew he would be a dandy in one more year. So, you've passed up that
good buck, but your family really enjoys eating deer meat. Near the end of
the bow season, you put a doe in the freezer.

Now a new bow season has just started. Since you've been seeing these
good bucks in a particular alfalfa field, you set a stand up near the edge of
that field. There is fresh sign, but after sitting there every evening for two
weeks, you haven't seen one good buck. What has happened?

Like I said, this scenario has happened to every bow hunter I know. Where do those bucks go? There may be several explanations. First, you aren't the only bowhunter who spotted those bucks in the alfalfa. Another bowhunter who works an 11 AM to 7 PM shift has been sitting on a stand on the other side of the field every morning. He hasn't seen much either, but his presence has added more human odor to the area.

Maybe the acorn mast was a good one and they have moved to some white oaks to feed during the daylight hours. After dark, they come to the alfalfa. But there is a more likely explanation. Come October, bucks, especially older bucks, become more nocturnal. They are still feeding in that alfalfa field, but only after dark. They appear after dark, and leave in the morning before dawn. It is what good bucks do.

There is one other possibility.

A camera study done in Missouri by Dr. Grant Woods suggests that as many as half the bucks over 2½ years of age leave their home range in late September and do not return for a year. These bucks move to an entirely new home range. It might only be 1000 yards from where they have been living — maybe just on the adjacent farm to where you've seen him in the past. Or maybe he moved as far as five miles from his original home range.

They note that some of these bucks return during the summer, but come the time when velvet is dropping from antlers, some leave again for the year. They believe that this home range shift is caused by a shift in preferred food sources. They move to find better food. If there is good rains and good forage, fewer bucks shift their home range.

Before moving on, let me give one other bit of interesting data from this Woods study. Based on the placement of many cameras in the field, they believe that often hunters will only get photos of 50-70 percent of bucks 2½ and 3½ years old that live in that area. The cameras will only get photos of 25 percent of those 4½ and older. Home range shifts could account for this in part, but we would add that the decrease in the size of the core home range as bucks age would also decrease the chance to get them on your field cameras.

The fact that as much as 50 percent of the older, mature bucks may leave your property in the fall is the bad news for you. The good news is that some older bucks may leave their home range and move into the area you've been hunting. That might explain the sightings of a really good buck in your area that no one saw the year before. Several years ago bowhunter Mike Beatty took the new world record buck with a bow. Here we had the biggest buck ever harvested with a bow, yet neither the farmer nor hunters who hunted on the farm where Mike harvested the buck had ever seen this buck before. No one. Not even Mike. That buck was 4½ years old when taken.

Let me add another example. My good bowhunting friend, Dennis Crabtree, from Ohio hunted this big buck (photo below) the whole bow season in 2006. I think he saw him three times and got him on film as well.

The buck was seen during the summer but come the fall, 2007, he was gone. I've had several guys tell me that the big buck they were hunting must have been poached because they disappeared over night. Others speculate that the big bucks just go totally nocturnal and that is why they aren't seen. Dennis didn't say think the buck was poached, but he began to question exactly what happened as the 2007 fall bow season progressed. With no sightings and no photos on cameras, he began to think something happened to the buck, until early December when he got him on film again, right where he was last year. One whole year, and then he was back. It happens all the time. They don't die, they just disperse to a new area, where they may stay, or return a year later. Makes hunting these old guys all the more interesting; and all the more challenging. The story doesn't end here, because four days after getting him on film, Dennis took this buck with his bow. Great buck too.

One obvious conclusion from the above data is that the larger your property, the less likely that bucks will move to areas you can't hunt. They still might move because of food shortages, but if your property is large enough, they will be available for you to hunt. Obviously this depends on how big your property is and how far these older bucks move for the year.

Core Home Range is Critical

A deer's home range is where he/she moves during normal feeding, bedding and mating activities. Most of us never give much thought to how home range impacts hunting. Sure, we've been curious about how big an area a bucks lives in. But we really don't focus on home range, even though it can be very important. If you are seriously hunting one particular buck, knowing his home range can be an advantage when scouting an area. There are some parts of that range, such as a good funnel between his bedding and feeding areas that may allow an encounter. Then there are other parts of the home range where the buck will catch you every time.

This radio-collared buck was one of 25 mature bucks Zaiglin and Demarais studied on a large conventional fenced ranch in South Texas. The average home range for mature deer in this study was 3,000 acres.

One rule of thumb is that the home range of does is about one-third the size of bucks. Another rule of thumb is that the better the food, and security cover, the smaller the home range. That makes sense to me.

Although intensive camera studies can help track down deer, radio collars are the key research tools that allows biologists to pin point individual buck home ranges. Researchers now have something called activity collars, which add another dimension to following deer. With those collars the biologist can determine if the buck is moving or inactive. Throw in satellites that allow continual monitoring via computers, and now you know exactly where that deer is, and what he is doing, 24 hours a day.

One concept that some researchers have utilized in the past few years sheds a lot of light on where you should be hunting. That concept is called "core" home range. *The core home range is where a buck spends 50 percent of his time.* And the reason this is valuable is because the core home range for older bucks is about ten times smaller than his entire home range. Clearly, knowing where that is can greatly help you when hunting. In fact, knowing the core home range for an individual buck you are hunting is almost necessary. If you get into that area, chances are he will be there (he is there half of his time), and if you bust him, it's over for the year. You really need to know where that range is so you don't stray into it by mistake.

Let me digress just a minute while on this subject of the core home range. Knowing where the core home range is critical to your success, and this means that scouting is also extremely important. You can use cameras, and they are extremely helpful in telling you what is out there. But nothing beats pounding the brush, especially in the winter, spring, and summer prior to hunting season. Finding the bedding and feeding areas of an individual buck pretty much tells you where the core home range is. Of course there are a ton of variables, one being that come the fall, foods change and the core home range does as well. Knowing where the white oak trees, and acorns, are, relative to one individual buck, is just another "piece of the puzzle."

Now let's get into this discussion of the home range on deer and how it can improve your success.

Before we start, note this basic fact about shape of the home range. Dr. James Kroll in Texas has done a lot of work on home range, and his data show that most deer home ranges are not circular, but elliptical.

Streams, ridgelines, roads (which deer do not tend to cross), all cause deer home ranges to be elliptical in shape. Maybe not critical information, but interesting.

Does Home Range and "Core" Home Range Size Vary During The Year?

Perhaps the best research done on home range and deer movements within their home range is a Master's Thesis completed in 2007 by James Tomberlin, at the 3,300-acre Chesapeake Farms in Maryland. Dr. Mark Conners is the wildlife manager there and worked with Jim and other graduate students on several studies on the eastern shore of Maryland.

Tomberlin followed fifteen adult bucks (all at least 2½ years of age; most older than that) during the summer (Aug 1-Sep 2), the early fall (Sep 3-Sep 23), two pre rut periods (Sep 24-Oct 14; Oct 15-Nov 4), the rut (Nov 5-20), the post rut (Nov 21-Dec 30), and the winter (Dec 17-Jan 6). They were able to get home ranges for three bucks in 2003, three in 2004 and 9 in 2005. Combining all bucks for all months, the average home range was 740 acres and the "core" home range 100 acres.

But, there were obvious differences by month and by periods. The largest home ranges were found in the peak rut (741 acres, with a core home range of 115 acres) and right before the rut (Oct 15-Nov 4, 706 acres). The summer home ranges averaged 284 acres, and as forage declined, bachelor groups broke up, and rutting behavior started, the home range sizes increased. For example they found that one buck's home range in August was 300 acres, but it increased to 1,000 acres by November. In August his core home range was only 30 acres, but it jumped to 120 acres in October and 150 acres in November. Note however, *for all bucks, the core home range was never over 14 percent of the home range.* Hence, a good rule of thumb for deer in the Northeast (and maybe into the Midwest) is that bucks spend half their time in an area around 15 percent the size of their entire home range. Thus, it is essential that you find the bedding and feeding areas for bucks you are hunting. Once done, you now know where that buck is 50 percent of the time.

Summer home ranges averaged 284 acres for all bucks, and their core range for that period was 35 acres. Obviously good feed was present at that time and they didn't have to move much to find it. If you can manage your

At 10 years of age (based on tooth wear), this South Texas radio-collared buck developed a 188-inch rack, but more importantly demonstrated an extremely small home range during the five years it was collared.

property so there is good security bedding cover close to good food plots, then bucks won't move much at this time of the year. You might say, "so what?" One obvious benefit to deer that don't have to move much to find good bedding areas and good feeding areas is less exposure to predation, automobiles, etc.

Tomberlin also noted individual variation in home ranges by month and age. For example one 2½ year-old buck had a home range of 487 acres in August, and a core home range of 57 acres. In September his home range went up to 756 acres, and his core home range was 82 acres. In October he ranged 793 acres, but spent half his time in 151 acres. In November he covered 929 acres, but spent half his time in 143 acres, and in December he covered 892 acres, with half his time spent in 163 acres. Interestingly he had three different core home ranges during that time.

Compare these figures to that of a 4½ year-old buck that would score in the 150's. His home range in August was 353, but his core home range was 30 acres. In September his home range was 227 acres, and his core was 32; October was 568 acres and 72 acres; November was 1070 and 146; and December was 810 and 171. Comparing these two bucks we note that *the older buck had the smallest home range and core home range*. We also note that both bucks covered more ground in the rut and post rut.

Tomberlin found that during a drought in 2001, does spent 50 percent of their summer time activity in corn. His data also showed data that during the rut, on rather rare occasions, some does leave their home range for a day or two, walk in a rather straight line to a selected spot, stay there awhile then come back home. He speculated that these does were actively seeking bucks during the rut. Does looking for bucks? Interesting.

The conclusion of this Maryland study is that home range size increases from August to November and the core home range is less than 15 percent of the home range (speculation was that the core home range was small because food availability on the farm was excellent). In fact, this brings up

Dispersal by yearling males is a common event in the wild, yet dispersal varies dependent on habitat. Thicker forrested habitat yields shorter dispersal distances than open farmland.

a definite characteristic of home ranges in deer. *The better the habitat, the smaller the home range.* They also conclude that there is a lot of individual variation in home range size especially in older bucks. Finally they noted a shorter, smaller lull in mid day movements in November.

Does Buck Home Range Size Decrease As They Age?

Dr. Mickey Hellickson, who works at the King Ranch in Texas, is conducting some of the most innovative deer movement research in the country. Over the past eight years he and his cohorts have collared thousands (yes, thousands) of bucks and followed their movements from one year to the next in South Texas. He has the advantage of doing the on-going research where buck harvest is limited to bucks 5½ years of age and older, so there is good survival of bucks to that age. Thus, for some individuals he has home range data when they were 1½ years old and the same when they were at least 5½ years old. The results are extremely interesting.

One final point before we present the results. A number of yearling bucks disperse, leaving their original home range. These data are included in the home range sizes, so yearling bucks seem to have very large home ranges, but remember, they had a birth home range then they move several miles away as yearlings and set up a permanent home range where they remain sometimes for life. The data presented on home range for 1½ year-old bucks includes both. In addition, 15% of bucks 2½ years of age and older dispersed from their home range, which escalates the size of the home range for most bucks in that age category. In other northern studies the dispersal rate for 2-year-old bucks was around 10 percent.

Now to the results. Dr. Hellickson found that as bucks age, their home ranges get smaller. For example, the home range for 1½ year-old bucks was 1,028 acres; at 5½ it decreased their home ranges by 56% to 449 acres, and at 6½ the home range decreased to 146 acres.

Once bucks dispersed, did they *move* their home ranges as they aged? Not really. From one year to the next there was a 61-63 percent overlap in home ranges of bucks from 1½ years to 7½ years of age. After dispersal, the distance from the center of the home range of yearling bucks to the center of the home range for those same bucks when they were 4½ years of age or older, was 1,379 yards. That's 300 or so yards less than a mile.

If you throw out data for the 15% of bucks that dispersed after age 2½, then the distance between the center of where they lived at 1½ to where they lived at 4½ or older, was only 579 yards. Bottom line, at least for Texas, is that once a buck reaches 2½ years of age, his home range doesn't move much. He will be centered less than one mile from where he was at 2½ years and he will be there till he dies.

Dr. Hellickson also found something else that should interest hunters. The home range of deer is where they spend all of their time. In other words, if you take all of the radio locations taken for a buck during the fall season, or maybe just for one month, you will have the home range of that deer for that period. But if you plot the radio locations of where bucks spend 50% of their time (we call that the *core home range*), you will have a much smaller area. For example, you will remember that for all bucks over 4½ years of age, the home range was 535 acres. Interestingly the core home range was only 89 acres.

Because of dispersal and the subsequent larger home ranges, the authors concluded that it was not possible to manage all bucks born on one area throughout their life. In fact it would take 2,500 acres to contain 55 percent of bucks 2½ to 4½ years of age. That same acreage would hold 83 percent of bucks over 4½ years of age. The authors of that study note that as properties become more irregular in shape, fewer deer will be able to remain entirely on the property.

Obviously the core home range is where the bucks bed and feed. This area is critical for the hunter, because older bucks are in those 89 acres

Even in ideal habitat, the South Texas study conducted by Demarais and Zaiglin recorded home ranges up to 10,000 acres for some mature bucks, demonstrating how unpredictable old bucks can be.

over half of their time. You want to around the core home range, but not in it. Knowing the core home range allows you to focus on a much smaller area when hunting older bucks. This is a super advantage.

Core home ranges also decreased with age. The core home range size for yearling bucks was 250 acres, but those same bucks only had a core home range of 55 acres by the time they were 5½ years of age (a 78% decrease).

Dr. Mark Conners at Chesapeake Farm in Maryland has done similar work on home ranges of does. That farm has great feed and good cover. In short, it is superior habitat for deer. We know that great habitat leads to much smaller home ranges. Dr. Conners found that some does had a home range of only 100 acres, and during the fall their core home range was only 15 acres.

So again, as we said before, if you have good habitat, deer don't move much. This holds for does as well as bucks.

There is one other factor related to home range. Research shows that some bucks don't read the books. Some individual older bucks cover four times as much ground as other bucks, and have much larger home ranges. We've noted that at several places in this book; bucks have a lot of individual variation. That concept also applies to the size of home range.

All data do not show that home ranges get smaller as bucks age. Some limited data from Minnesota shows the fall home range of a buck increased each of his first three years. They also showed that bucks dispersed at all ages, sometimes returning to their birth home range. Most didn't stay there very long and returned to their new home range. Another study done in Illinois showed buck home ranges to be in the 1000-acre range as opposed to the smaller areas found in Texas. Makes sense though when you think about all the open farm land in Illinois, interspersed with small fragments of forest. The other factor here may be deer density. We know that the higher the density the smaller the home range. I'd say that on average Texas has a higher deer density than Illinois.

Let's try to tie this all together. Home ranges and core home ranges vary, but are much smaller in good habitat. Since bucks are inactive a lot of the time, and are active and available to the hunter at dawn and dusk most of the year, it is critical to find the core home range. Finding the core home range of a buck means finding bedding and feeding areas. All you then have to do is pick a good spot between the two and hammer them. Hmmm. If only it was that easy.

Does Rain Impact Home Range Size?

Yes, definitely. In Texas, rains are critical and in good years, with better food, home ranges are smaller. There was also a four-year study where radio-collared deer were tracked in the coastal plain of South Carolina. The key was rainfall. In years of low rain, home ranges were much larger, apparently because food supplies were lower forcing deer to move.

Hunter: *I hunt with some guys on 1,000 acres. How many of the bucks born on my area will be there when they get old? In other words, if I protect the yearling bucks, will they leave and get shot on the neighbor's property where they shoot anything that has antlers, regardless of size?*

Dave/Bob: *Great question. Hellickson looked at this for ranches in South Texas. Using his data that we quote in this chapter, he found that 55 percent of bucks 2½ to 4½ years of age would be found on property that was approximately 2500 acres in size all the time. For bucks over that age, 83 percent would be on that same property all the time. Since most of us don't have properties of that size to hunt, and to manage then, your bucks will spend some time on adjacent properties.*

Hunter: *You state that the better the habitat, the smaller the home range. I own 250 acres where I hunt deer. What should I be doing to get the bucks to stay on my property?*

Dave/Bob: *With that size property, you can't keep all the bucks on there all the time. But if you can create good food, via food plots, and some thick security sanctuary cover, then you decrease the size of not only the buck's home range, but also his core home range. We feel that thick-cover sanctuaries are very important. As much as ten percent of your land should be thick sanctuary habitat to keep things stable. These areas should be off limits to humans at all times (except when following a wounded buck). In fact, if you can stay away from the edges of these sanctuaries, all the better. What you want is for bucks on property around your area to come to these sanctuaries when they are pressured, and to feel secure there.*

Hunter: *Is there anything else I can do to help hold deer on my hunting lands?*

Dave/Bob: *Yes there is. Keep human activity to a minimum. This is critical. Let's use this example. You have 700 acres, a river on one side, a four-lane highway on another side, and private land on the third side owned by a widower who is an anti-hunter. The fourth side of your property is a farm where hunting occurs. You practice quality deer management and have good bucks on your property. How do you reduce human activity? You might only allow bowhunting. Quiet, and doesn't disturb deer. You might have a road that goes around the perimeter of the property, and all hunting is then done on foot. You walk to all stands from that road. You do not allow any drive hunting; it must be stand or blind hunting with some spot and stalk. All of the above keep noise and human pressure to a minimum and give the bucks a feeling of security on your land. Thus, if you have the thick cover and food, you will attract bucks and with low human pressure, they will stay.*

CHAPTER 9

Understand
Why Deer Move

There is a fair amount of literature, both popular and scientific, that discusses the factors that affect deer movement. The problem is that there are a lot of variables that can affect deer movement, and this complicates most scientific studies. These variables include; hormones and breeding, food, moon phase, human pressure, wind, temperature, barometric pressure, buck to doe ratio, dispersal, etc. The list goes on and on, and we can't begin to cover it all. So what we have tried to do is look at the science and present the results of what researchers have found relative to many of these variables and deer movement.

One problem is that one study done in one location gives different results on the same variable as another study done somewhere else. Part of the problem is that when studying one variable (such as deer movement and temperature) the results may become clouded because of other variables (such as barometric pressure or the moon cycle) acting at the same time. We can speculate about the results and the differences in results from studies done in two different areas, but it is just speculation.

the science and leave the interpretations up to you. Of all the

; book, this was the hardest to collate simply because deer

don't talk. Still, we believe there are some things in here that almost certainly can help you better understand why deer move. And knowing why they move may well help you to understand when and where they will move.

At the 2006 Quality Deer Management Association's annual convention, there were several interesting presentations on deer movement. Dr. Mark Conners presented data on deer movements on Chesapeake Farms on the eastern shore of Maryland. He looked at the travel distance by time of day and found the peak time for deer movement was 5-7 AM and in the evening. No surprise here.

In August he found that in the AM, bucks moved about 330 yards, with little movement in the day, then movement of 435 yards in the evening. In October he found they moved between 330 and 650 yards in the morning

Deer movements are dictated by a number of factors, none more important than open water in the semi arid region of South Texas, particularly in drought when deer are forced to concentrate around the depleting resource. This then makes them more susceptible to predators.

and 220 to 330 yards in the evening, but there was a lot of individual variation in daily movements at this time. Come November the individual buck movements were highly variable. Some moved a lot more than others. And some bucks moved continually throughout the day. More on this study in a minute.

Dr. Mickey Hellickson gave a paper on deer movements at that same convention and noted that there are two major factors that affect movement regardless of the weather: the need to breed, and the need to feed. Obviously deer must do both, but there is no doubt that weather and other variables affect the need to breed and the need to feed. We shall present Dr. Hellickson's information, and that of others in this chapter. Hopefully you will find some gems that will allow you to be more successful.

Does Weather Determine Whether They Move?

Excuse our play on words, but among hunters there is a lot of discussion on weather and deer movement. We're going to start this part of the chapter with some very recent, and interesting, data from South Texas.

Dr. Mickey Hellickson put motion-sensitive collars on 43 bucks in South Texas in areas where there was little hunting pressure (ranches where only bucks 5½-years-old or older could be harvested). These collars allowed him to not only know where the bucks were, but whether they were moving or not. He assigned the bucks into four age classes, and noted their movements as being inactive (bedded, standing) or active (feeding, walking, running). He followed these bucks 24 hours a day during the pre-rut (Oct 1-Nov 31) and the rut (Dec 1-Jan 10), collecting data for six consecutive years. With this super data he correlated buck movements to various weather-related variables.

Based on his data and observations, Dr. Hellickson believes that deer movement is caused by the two basic factors mentioned above. The first

At no time are bucks more active than right before the peak of the rut.

is their need to breed. For bucks, testosterone is the driving force that gets them into breeding condition. The second factor is their need to feed. These two factors determine why and when they move. Weather, moon, human pressure, buck to doe ratio, and other things can enter in, but when it comes to deer movement, these are the keys.

Let's look at the interesting trends that Dr. Hellickson found. First, *57 percent of the time, bucks are inactive.* This means that over half the time they are either bedded or standing in one spot. Assuming that 30 percent of that is bedding at night, there is another one-quarter of the 24 hour day when they are fairly inaccessible to you. This explains why we don't have bucks running around under our tree stands or near our ground blinds all the time. When you look at the big picture it becomes obvious that bucks don't move around all that much. If he is bedded or not moving (as they are 57 percent of the time in South Texas), you aren't going to see him. We can spot and stalk them, but that is not done all that much for deer. This bit of data tells us how important bedding areas are for deer. This is very important. The closer you can set up to those areas without buggering them, the better chance you have of seeing a buck when he is active.

The second thing Dr. Hellickson found was that daytime movements peak when you thought they did; 7-9 AM and 6-7 PM. Third, on a yearly

On intensively hunted lands, bucks are primarily noctural; however, based on Zaiglin's research 50% of buck visits at scrapes occur under the protection of darkness even on landholdings with limited hunting pressure.

basis, deer are most active (move more) right before the peak of the rut and they are the least active in the spring. Fourth, *during the rut they tend to be active all day,* decreasing at night. Fifth, *the older a buck gets, the less he moves.* We discussed this a bit in the previous chapter. As noted in Chapter 8, not only do home ranges get smaller as bucks age, their core home range (where bucks spend 50% of their time) gets really small. We'll talk more on that later.

Sixth, young and middle-aged bucks move more than mature or old bucks. His seventh finding is most interesting. From observations made on movements of 43 different bucks, he found that *there is a lot of individual variation in buck movements.* In fact, *he found that some bucks move four times more than other bucks.* For example, remembering that all bucks are only active 43 percent of the time, he found one 6-½ year-old buck that was active 87 percent of the time, while an 8-½ year-old buck was only active 18 percent of the time. Thus, they are a lot like people. There are some older guys who walk every day, climb mountains, and are just plain active, and others who sit around and watch TV a lot.

Dr. Randy DeYoung also found a big variation in the amount that bucks move during the rut. Some stay within their home range and move a lot. Others stay within their home range and move very little. And some older bucks leave their home range and set up a new range, staying for several days to months, then return to their original home range. Finally, some bucks move out of their home range just during the peak of the rut, stay a few days, then return. The conclusion is that bucks do not always read the book, and individual variations in movements during the breeding season are common. That might explain why your scouting trips gave you great optimism, only to be dashed by reality once the hunting season started. Where did they go?

This individual variation in behavior of bucks also shows up in breeding behavior. In Chapter 10, we'll talk more about this. For example, *some old bucks don't mate does at all.* Other, scrubby old bucks that have poor antlers and low weight mate more than big, older bucks. What's that all about? I'm not sure but it shows that individual variation in buck mating behavior occurs more than we ever suspected. Same for buck movements.

Dr. James Kroll collected data in Texas and found that feeding activity was greatest in the late afternoon for bucks over 3-½ years of age. In fact, these older bucks moved less than other does and bucks, except for the late afternoon. One other point to make, Kroll compared deer activity from an area in Michigan to one in Texas and found that afternoon deer activity tended to start earlier in Michigan. He postulated that the hot Texas temperatures caused deer activity to occur later in the afternoon.

There is a fair amount of other data on temperature and deer movements. Again, the Hellickson study has data on this that is surprising to say the least. He found no correlation between temperature and deer movements. Remember though, this is South Texas. Even though there isn't a study with the type of data Mickey Hellickson collected, there are a few studies from the North that show that temperature is a factor for deer movement. In fact, Charles Alsheimer and others believe that in the fall, buck movements decrease sharply when you get above 45 degrees. Not so in South Texas.

Jim Tomberlin's thesis data from Maryland showed that buck activity decreased (especially in early morning) as the changes in hourly temperature increased in late September through the first week of November. But in the post-rut (Nov 26-Dec 16), buck activity increased as change in hourly temperature increased. Of interest is the fact that warm weather affected buck movement, *except* during the peak rut. During the peak rut you need to be hunting, regardless of how warm it might be.

Several years ago I was bowhunting in early November in Illinois. Daytime temperatures soared into the 80's, and buck sightings were low. On the third day, I asked the landowner where the coolest place was on his farm. He took me to a stream bottom in a small, but steep, ravine. When we hit the stream, it was almost dry. There was a trickle here and there, and a few small pockets of water, but very little moisture. However, as soon as we got to the stream bed, we noticed a temperature decrease. It was amazing. There had to be a 10 degree difference. We hadn't walked fifty yards down stream when a huge buck jumped from his bed in lose gravel right beside the water. I snuck in there before daylight the next morning and shot a dandy buck as he walked up the stream bottom.

Few will argue that unseasonable hot weather in the North, during the rut, will really curtail bucks movements during the day. They just avoid the heat. Charlie Alsheimer uses 45 degrees as a rule of thumb for deer movement in New York and elsewhere in the North. When it gets warmer than that, deer movement in November is curtailed. But there is still some movement.

When it's really, really cold, movements will also change. They will get out of the wind, spend time on sunny hillsides (especially those out of the wind), and become more active during the warmest parts of the day. In cold weather during the rut, there may be an exception. In my experience, when a nasty snow storm hits during the night, and the morning temperatures are cold, buck activity can be very good.

Now back to the Texas study. Hellickson also found only a very slightly negative correlation between humidity and movements and no correlation between barometric pressure and movements. Hellickson did not look at time lag, so that might explain these data. But, he also notes, and we agree, that this lack of correlation does not hold for more northerly areas. Cold fronts in the North bring colder temperatures, lower relative humidity and higher barometric pressure. In my experience, and that of most deer hunters, deer activity is high at this time, but drops once the front hits. Then, as things clear after the storm, deer activity really cranks up and you need to be out there.

Breeding core shifts are not uncommon and some deer move considerable distances to relocate during the rut.

What about rain?

There is almost no scientific data that looks at rain and deer movements and what little there is does not give a strong consensus. Hellickson found that a two-inch rain in September caused increased movements by 70 percent, while a one-inch October rain led to no increase in deer movements. These data are a bit contrary, and other variables may have come into play. Even so, it is obvious that there is much we don't know about rain and deer movements. My own experience is that a light rain or drizzle is a great time to hunt, especially during the rut.

If rains, even drizzly rains, continue for several days, then deer activity dwindles. And if you get a very heavy rain during the day, but with little wind, deer keep feeding. But if there are high winds, or if the rains are heavy at night, then I believe that buck activity slows considerably. Being a bowhunter, I quit when rains get heavy for several reasons; shooting the bow becomes difficult, and blood trails become non existent. However, right after heavy rains can be a great time to hunt. I believe that at that time deer want to feed, and rutting bucks want to freshen up scrapes.

As opposed to South Texas where weather doesn't seem to be a major factor in deer movements, in more northerly climates weather is a factor. But there are lots of variables. We all grew up believing that approaching cold fronts stimulate deer to feed. Perhaps this isn't as much a factor in October, but come cold weather, it does sound logical. It works for humans. When the weather prognosticators predict an approaching snow storm, the local food markets fill up quickly.

The same seems to be true for deer. Most hunters believe a cold snap triggers rut behavior, however, outdoor writer Jeff Murray believes that the

Some bucks, referred to as unkillable (normally trophy-caliber bucks), hypothetically avoid the intense rut and remain sedentary, moving only after the rut is over.

cold snap isn't what causes this movement. Rather the darker conditions from overcast skies followed by a bright sky jump starts the deer. Both ideas make sense.

The Rut; Where Do Those Bucks Go?

In Chapter 8 we discussed the studies done following 15 radio-collared bucks at Chesapeake Farms in Eastern Maryland. The key study was James Tomberlin's Master's Thesis done while a student at North Carolina State University. Remember, Tomberlin followed deer in two pre-rut periods (Sep 24-Oct 14, Oct 15-Nov 4), the rut (Nov 5-Nov 25), and the post-rut (Nov 26-Dec 16). The results are interesting to say the least.

We noted in Chapter 8 that some older bucks just pull up stakes and move after the velvet drops from their antlers. They may stay in their new home range a whole year and then return to the original home range. Or they may just come back to visit their original home range. Either way, it explains in part why some bucks you've been hunting just up and disappear. It also explains why you may see a big buck on your area, which you have never seen before. The reason? He wasn't there before and he just moved in.

The Tomberlin study in Maryland spent considerable effort looking at buck movements during the rut. Turns out that all bucks don't just have one home range. Take "40 orange" for example. This 4½-year-old buck had two home ranges over 1.2 miles apart. In the summer, he lived in one home range, but from Sep 3 to Sep 23, he used both areas. After that he moved to the second home range.

Before Sep 24 "22 blue" (age unknown) lived in one area, but he then shifted and used both his original home range and a new home range 1.7 miles away. But by October 15, his core home range was in the new area, and most of his home range was there as well, but he still spent a little time at the original location. Come the rut (Nov 5) and into the post rut he spent all his time in the new home range. No wonder such bucks are hard to hunt.

Buck "49 blue" (age 3½ years) didn't shift home ranges. However, he used two different areas that were 3.7 miles apart. During the summer and also from Nov 26 to Dec 10, he used one area. But during Sept 3-Sep 23 and Oct 15- Nov 25, and after Dec 10, he used both areas. He made purposeful movements from one area to the other on three different occasions. The first was on Sep 7 and he stayed until Sep 23; the second was on Oct 20 and he stayed until Nov 18. His third trip to the other home range was Dec 27 to Dec 29.

Question, *do bucks leave their home range for an extensive movement, to areas not previously occupied?* The answer to this question is "yes." Tomblinson's study is very enlightening on this topic especially since he has pre-rut, rut, post-rut, and winter data.

Table 1.

Percent of bucks that leave their home range for an extensive movement. Data from 15 bucks, all over 2½ years of age.

	% of bucks that move from their home range	day time mvmt.	night time mvmt.
Sep 24-Oct 14	13%	0%	100%
Oct 15-Nov 4	40%	30%	70%
Nov 5-Nov 25	58%	73%	27%
Nov 26-Dec 16	20%	30%	70%
Dec 17-Jan 6	17%	Unknown	Unknown

As you look at Table 1, note that four of the 15 bucks monitored in this study were 5½ years-old, five were 4½, two were 3½, and four were of unknown age. But all bucks were over 2½ years of age. No one has ever published this type of data and it is most interesting and explains why some of the bucks you hunt disappear for a day or more. The reason is that some older bucks leave their home range for excursions into new territory. We can't tell from this table how often bucks move out of their home range during each time period, we just know that they did leave. For example, during the rut (Nov. 5 - Nov. 25) 58 percent of the bucks left their home range at least once. Some may have left more than once, but we don't have that information.

The thesis did not specify how long these bucks stayed in the new area, but I believe that most returned within a day. This means you can be hunting an area that you have thoroughly scouted and see a big buck that you have never seen before, and, you may never see him again. Or you can be on a big buck, having seen him three days in a row at the same area, move your stand to that spot, and strike out. He may have moved out for a day, and then return.

Note from Table 1 that as you move from the pre-rut to the rut, more and more bucks take these short-time excursions out of their home range. Then, after the rut, those percentages go down again. The second interesting bit of data here is *when* the bucks depart their home range. The sample size is small during the Sep 24-Oct 14 period. But in the pre-rut (Oct 15-Nov 4) 70 percent of such movements are at night. Come the rut, 73 percent of such movements are during the day. So in the rut, 58 percent of older bucks move out of your area for a little while (which also means that a bunch of older bucks move into your area from their original home range), and they make many of these excursions during the day. This explains why bucks you've never seen pop up under your tree stand during the rut. Then in the post rut, excursions again take place after dark. If you ever needed data to show you why you need to hunt all day during the rut, this is it. And, in fact, these data give you good reason to also spend a lot of time out there before (Oct. 15 - Nov. 4) and after the rut (Nov. 26 - Dec. 16) as 30 percent of their extensive movements occur during the day.

The Moon, Rut Activity and Deer Movements

Here's a topic that generates discussion and dialogue in every deer camp when there is a full moon. Does it hurt, does it help, and are we wasting our time hunting in the day? The questions go on and on. As you read this section, you will see that there is some science, but there are lots of bits and pieces of a puzzle that are difficult to put together. We'll present them as best we can, and let you pull out what you need. The real truth, relative to hunting the rut and the affects of the moon on buck movement, is that even though no one knows all the answers, there is a three-week period every year when you just need to be out there, regardless of lunar phases. Let's be honest. Come the first of November, few hunters look at lunar tables, or the phase of the moon and say, "I'd hunt today, but the lunar tables say that tomorrow is better, so I'll just sit by the fire," or, "I'm not going out today because there is too much moon at night." They just hunt.

Most wildlife biologists believe that the decreasing amount of day light (compared to darkness) in the fall kicks off rutting behavior. This decreasing light is known as photoperiod. Now if this is what kicks off the rut, then the timing of the rut, i.e. the peak of the rut, will be the same, or roughly so, every fall, because photoperiod is the same every fall.

Although the peak is the same, in some years it may not appear the same because the intensity at the peak can vary. Let's assume that it is late October and warm. Then a cold snap occurs, and you see an eruption of scrapes and rubs, and some chasing as well. For example, let's then suppose that come the normal time for the peak, around November 10th or so, the weather warms up, and the amount of rutting activity slows. So, even though the peak of the rut is still November 10th-15th, the low intensity makes it appear that the peak occurred at a different time.

Thus, conventional thinking is that decreasing day length is the key to deer movements due to rutting behavior. However, there are several hunters and outdoor writers who believe that it is the moon in combination with photoperiod that causes the timing of rut to vary each year. These hunters have several ideas as to how the moon affects the timing of the rut.

The idea that the sun and/or moon affect the rut and deer movement is nothing new. There is a very interesting, and somewhat complex, book on natural clocks and natural rhythms in animals. In *"Biological Time"*, published in 2004, Bernie Taylor discusses how early man used the moon to determine when to hunt. Those beliefs carry over to today. Charles Alsheimer, Jeff Murray, and Dave Morris have written a lot about the moon and the rut. "Goggle" their names and find several books that go into all of this in great detail.

Another truth is that scientific studies don't give us a consensus on impacts of the moon on buck activity. Some studies have shown no relationship and others show that deer move more at night with a full moon. Space does not permit us to get into great detail on every moon theory, so we'll just quickly summarize them. For example, Jeff Murray has written about the earth's gravitational pull, and how moon position impacts the rut. He believes that deer movement is highest when the moon is directly overhead or directly underfoot. We know that deer are most active at dawn and dusk so if you can pinpoint the days of the month when the moon is in either of the aforementioned positions at dawn and dusk, you theoretically have the best days to hunt. Interesting idea, but we do not know of any scientific studies that confirm or reject this theory.

Then there is the moon phase theory promoted by good friend Charles Alsheimer and Wayne LaRoche. They believe that the phase of the moon contributes to the influence that photoperiod (amount of day light) has on the rut.

To fully understand this, let's first list some basic lunar time lines. The first official day of fall (called the autumnal equinox) occurs

on September 21. The full moon that is closest to the equii
as the "harvest" moon and the next full moon is known as \
moon. Since the moon reflects light it receives from the sun,
the moon, the sun, and the earth, cause the cycles of the moon. The new
moon (completely dark) occurs when the moon is between the sun and the
earth. This prevents light from being reflected, so it is a dark moon. At this
time the moon rises at dawn and sets at dusk. Seven days later, we reach
the first quarter (half moon). Over the next few days the moon grows and
a week later we reach full moon (completely bright). Full moons rise at
dusk and set and dawn. Now the cycle goes the other way with a shrinking
moon. Seven days after the full moon we reach the last quarter (half moon)
when the moon is overhead at sunrise. Seven days later we start the cycle
all over again.

Alsheimer and LaRoche believe that the "hunter's" moon triggers
chasing and that peak breeding begins ten days after the "hunter's" moon.
(Usually the "hunter's" moon occurs in November, but not always).
Alsheimer's book, *Hunting Whitetails by the Moon*, makes a good case
for his theory. Dr. James Kroll also believes that the "hunter's" moon cues
does to come into estrus and that the peak of the rut will follow the full
moon. When you read his most interesting book, *Solving The Mysteries
of Deer Movement*, it does make sense. If you are interested in why deer
move, and moon phases, this book is worth reading. Dr. Kroll also showed
that the highest daytime activity is seven days from the new moon to the
first quarter (half moon). David Morris believes that there is more deer
movement during the new moon in early morning and late afternoon. For a
full moon he believes that most movement is at night, with some movement
spread out over mid day. But he notes one exception. When a full moon
coincides with the peak of the rut (2nd-3rd week in much of the northern
United States) Morris believes that the rutting behavior is increased, and
there is more movement during the day.

Various well known hunters have commented about the above lunar implications and they also have opinions about the many variables that influence deer movements making it hard to pinpoint lunar cycles as the cause. For example, noted deer hunter and outdoor writer Bill Winke, believes that there is merit to Alsheimer's theory.

The moon rises 50 minutes later each day in the fall and the Drury brothers believe that bucks move more during the time of day when the moon is rising. (You can find out exactly what time the moon rises each day by going to www.stargazing.net/kepler/moonrise.html).

Are there data on any of these theories relative to the timing of the rut and deer movement? Yes, there is some anecdotal information and you might check Dr. Kroll's above-cited book for some interesting data from Texas and Louisiana.

Robert Sheppard is a hunter from Alabama who kept detailed records on deer sightings and moon phase at three hunting lodges and published them in *Deer & Deer Hunting* magazine. Interestingly, he reported more deer seen during the full moon (5.0 per hunter per day), 3.7 for the new moon, 3.7 for the first quarter, and 3.6 for the last quarter. John Ozoga, biologist working within a one-square mile enclosure in Michigan, has written several articles on deer movements and the rut in his regular column in *Deer & Deer Hunting* magazine. He compared the breeding dates of deer in his enclosure to the lunar cycles, concluding that there was no affect. Dr. James Kroll found that in northern Louisiana, does had their lowest activity around the full moon and the most activity around the new moon.

Drs. Roseberry and Woolf at Southern Illinois University looked at lunar tables and found no association with buck activity. Researchers at the University of Georgia looked at moon phase and known breeding dates (from captive deer, and by measuring fetuses that can then be back-dated to give the approximate time of conception) from deer in Georgia, Mississippi, South Carolina, Texas, Missouri, Virginia, Maine, Michigan, and Minnesota.

There is an inverse relationship between human activity and deer movements.
Mature bucks respond by becoming nocturnal or
by selecting dense cover to avoid man.

They then compared conception dates with lunar phases and with the old method of using a calendar date based on photoperiod and slight weather variables that might influence peak breeding.

For example, they looked at the average breeding date for over one thousand does over a 13-year period in South Carolina and found the average breeding date was October 27, 6½ days before the "hunter's" moon. For those one thousand does there was only an average deviation of 4.6 days from October 27. The "hunter's" moon varies from year to year, so they looked at the average date of conception for individual years and compared that to the time of the "hunter's" moon and found a deviation of 11.4 days. They concluded that moon phase prediction of peak breeding dates was highly variable, while the tried-and-true calendar date method (i.e. decreasing day length) was much less variable.

The University of Georgia authors believed that, "It is not necessary to revise the conventional understanding among deer biologists that mean breeding dates are primarily influenced by photoperiod and are relatively consistent among years within a particular population."

James Tomberlin's thesis done in Maryland showed that older bucks were more active and moved around more during the pre-rut when we were in the dark phases of the moon.

Dr. Mickey Hellickson has collected the hardest data on the impacts of the moon on deer movements. As mentioned earlier in this chapter, he put motion-sensitive collars on 43 bucks in South Texas. He categorized deer movements as "inactive" (bedded, standing), or "active" (feeding, walking, running) and followed buck movements 24 hrs a day. He looked at movements during peak rut time from 1999 to 2005 and noted that only 2 of 6 peaks fell within the "hunter's" moon predictive period. He then looked at whether bucks move more at night during the full moon as has been speculated by many. He compared movements from 4-5 days of the full moon to 4-5 days around the new moon and looked at two years of data. He found no difference in buck movements.

Dr. Hellickson also compared the amount of day movements for these bucks during full moon vs. new moon and again found no differences. Just a note here. This South Texas data is most interesting and some of the best data ever collected on buck movements. Note though that there was very little hunting pressure in the area studied. Also note that for weather, barometric pressure, etc.—factors that affect deer movements—South Texas is considerably different than the North. Are potential movements dictated by the moon differently in South Texas? We don't know.

The Human Factor.
Does Hunting Pressure Cause Deer
To Change Movement Patterns?

For years we've heard that human hunting pressure causes deer to become more nocturnal. There is no question about this. Humans have a major impact on deer movement. Charlie Alsheimer has looked at deer movements on his New York property and that of his neighbors for many years. Using cameras, he showed that on lands where hunters were using quality deer management, and being very selective in the harvest of bucks (i.e. passing up lots of small bucks), 58 percent of deer activity during the rut occurred in daylight. On lands where there was heavy human activity, lots of hunters, only 32 percent of deer activity was in the day.

Recent new data out of Tennessee was collected on a piece of leased property where there were good buck sightings and harvests for several years, then things went sour. It turns out that hunters had gotten used to hunting certain tree stands over and over, year after year. The good bucks

Following the rut, bucks must replenish the energy resources depleted while pursuing does and will relocate to areas near food plots to replenish their bodies worn from rutting activities.

figured that out, so when the hunters moved to other areas on the lease, buck sightings and harvests again came back. The big boys were there all the time; they just figured out human behavior.

Mickey Hellickson and others from the University of Georgia and Texas A&M University at Kingsville had radio collars on 136 males. (This is a different Hellickson study, and yes Mickey Hellickson does a lot of deer research). They observed the behaviors of bedded bucks approached downwind by humans during the day. Locations were mapped for each male around forty minutes after they were chased from their beds. Bucks 2½-years-old traveled the greatest distance while bucks 4½ and 9½-years-old traveled the shortest distances. In general, the older the buck, the less distances they moved when disturbed.

There have been several studies that looked at deer movements before, during, and after a gun hunt and showed the value of good thick cover to keep bucks on your hunting area. One study was conducted on the Fair Hill Natural Resource Management Area in Maryland where there were 134 deer/square mile. Whoa. They obviously need to harvest deer there, so every year 75 hunters per day utilize assigned stands during a two-day hunt.

The problem is that even with this yearly hunt, deer numbers stayed the same, so researchers were looking for a reason. They followed radio-collared deer before, during, and after the hunt. Daytime movement for adult does before the hunt was around 390 yards. During the hunt does moved 430 yards each day, and immediately after the hunt they moved 270 yards. Bucks moved 430 yards a day before the hunt, 325 during the hunt and 780 after the hunt. Peak movement for both sexes occurred at night right after the hunt (does moved 560 yards, bucks moved 1000 yards). Obviously hunting pressure affected deer movements.

Of key interest was the discovery that some deer went to several "refuges" within the Management Area, one being a rather impenetrable (for hunters, not deer) multi-flora rose thicket. During and after the hunt a number of deer moved into these refuges. Once in that thick cover, telemetry showed that deer moved about one-third less than deer outside those refuges, especially during the hunt. Thus, they were much less vulnerable to being harvested by hunters. This proves the common sense belief that during hunting season, especially with guns, thick, sanctuary cover will attract, hold and protect bucks (and does) on your property.

Now let's discuss one more interesting study that shows that deer can be out there, but hunters don't harvest them because the hunters stay close to roads. It seems obvious that to more efficiently harvest deer, hunters must get away from roads to the rugged, steeper, forested, areas where deer live. But do they? Researchers at Penn State University issued GPS units to follow hunters on a large tract (113,048 acres) of public land. They then interviewed these same hunters. Remember that as they interviewed the hunters to ask where they hunted, the researchers already knew the answers. GPS results showed that hunters don't get far from roads. While they walked 3.4 miles during the day, they only hunted an average of 0.52 miles from a road. In fact 87% of deer hunters hunted within 0.3 miles of a road. From personal interviews, hunters felt they were hunting over a mile from a road, but the GPS data tell the story.

These data show that there are de facto refuges on public lands simply because hunters don't get there even when roads are relatively close to such areas. This research leads to the question of whether recreational hunting can be an effective tool for controlling deer on large tracts of public lands that are forested and contain steep terrain. Maybe not. In fact the authors suggest that in forested ravine habitats in Pennsylvania, deer hunters cannot control the herd. These data tell us that hunters need to move away from roads and get into those inaccessible spots to hunt. The deer are there and the hunters are not.

Food Affects Deer Movement

There is very little hard data to show that food plots, acorn trees, and other feeding areas affect deer movements, but we know they do. Sometimes such movements to and from food are affected by weather and other variables, but the need to feed definitely has a lot to do with deer movements.

Supplemental feed affects deer movements too and Dr. Harry Jacobson of Mississippi State University conducted a research project looking at this topic. He used automatic timers to document activity at feeding stations on the Circle Bar Ranch in Mississippi. They took 14,501 photos of feeding deer and showed what we all suspected - deer feed a lot after dark. (11,036 of the photos taken of feeding deer took place at night.) Deer begin to feed at 6:00 PM, but the peak feeding period was the first two hours after dusk (7:00-9:00 PM). They feed all night long, but have secondary peaks at 11:00 PM and again at 5:00 AM. During the early fall (when we are bowhunting) there is more late morning feeding (6:00-11:00 AM). Can we assume that deer feeding patterns are the same for natural food as for the artificial feed used in this study? Probably so. One last interesting note. Some very large bucks were photographed on this fenced ranch, but were NEVER seen by hunters. The big boys can hide.

Sex Ratios and Habitat Affects Movement

If sex ratios are not balanced, and there are tons of does out there, then the bucks cannot mate all does during one breeding cycle. Thus, 23-26 days later, when unbred does come into estrus again, we have bucks running around, chasing and tending does. But, via quality deer management, if you harvest larger numbers of does, bringing the sex ratio to a more natural, balanced situation, then more does will be bred within a shorter time period. This means that more does will drop in the spring, within a shorter time period and that helps fawn survival (predators can't get them all since they are dropped around the same time; you won't get as many late drops and late dropped fawns enter the following winter in lesser condition and have a higher chance of dying).

In essence then, when you get your buck-to-doe ratio in better shape several things happen that makes hunting better. You focus the rut into a shorter time period. This increases the intensity of the peak of the rut, and that means more fighting, more competition for does and more movement. How does this help you, the hunter? More competition for does means that bucks will respond more to rattling, calling, using decoys, etc. Think about it. If you have a ton of does out there, bucks don't need to come to rattling (where two bucks are fighting over a hot doe or in an area where there is a hot doe). They don't need to come to calls or decoys. Heck, they don't even need to come to scrapes, because there are so many hot does around that they just run into them all the time. It's true. The more does you have per adult buck, the less rubs and scrapes you will find in that area, simply because competition is not part of the equation.

Also when you kill more does, the habitat tends to improve and this also shortens the rut for the same reasons just cited above. So, for better hunting in the rut, and a whole lot more fun, *you definitely want the adult sex ratio to be between 1 doe per buck to 3 does per buck.*

Buck Dispersal

Here is something that almost every hunter has observed. In the fall, especially in October, you will see small bucks that you never saw before. You've hunted an area fairly hard, and think you have all the bucks in the area pegged, then come mid-October, here comes a bunch of new, but small, bucks. What's that all about?

The answer to this mystery is called "dispersal," and it occurs every fall when 50-90 percent of all yearling (1½ year-old) bucks emigrate out of their birth home range. They depart, and set up living quarters in a whole new area. Some bucks disperse in the spring, but most do so in the month prior to the rut. In my area, that's October. The distances they move varies with the habitat; the more forests, the less the dispersal distance. In forested areas the average dispersal distance is five miles, though some individuals go much further. In more open farm country the average dispersal distance is closer to fifteen miles. One study done in Illinois showed an average dispersal distance of 25 miles.

A Pennsylvania study showed that in forested areas the bucks dispersed in fairly straight line movements. They leave the area in which they were born and in two hours reach an area where they will spend the rest of their life. However, roads and rivers did seem to be a barrier. Often a new home range was established before a river or a two-lane, paved highway. On the average Pennsylvania dispersing bucks crossed just one paved road. They dispersed to a river or a paved road and stopped there. When bucks disperse they may be subjected to higher mortality as they move into areas that are new to them. Automobiles may hit some. Others may lose fights to bigger bucks. Maybe dispersal is meant to happen so that only the strongest survive?

While it is true that young bucks from one property leave, it is also true that the reverse also occurs as others move in. One reality is that the exchange of yearling migrant bucks may not be equal. Your property might be producing bucks with greater antler potential than the bucks that move in. If, for some reason, your area has very high emigration rates and those that move in have lower survival, there can be a net loss of yearling bucks. Yes, there is a lot we do not know about dispersal, but some new research is starting to cast light on this phenomenon.

In recent years there has been an increased emphasis on deer management strategies that include improving habitat, increasing doe harvests and protecting younger bucks. It's called quality deer management (QDM) and learning why bucks disperse may relate to such strategies (example: if dispersal is lower, you might keep more of those high-quality, younger bucks growing on your property). This leads us to the real question, *why do yearling bucks disperse?*

It is known that yearling bucks move out, even if the habitat is good. Thus, there are probably social pressures that are the cause. Maybe the mothers drive them out. A 1994 Illinois study showed no differences in dispersal rates for orphaned and non-orphaned male fawns. That might be true for open farm country, but it didn't hold for Virginia. There, a 1992 study showed that button bucks orphaned before they reached one year of age had much lower dispersal rates than those that stayed with their mother longer than one year. Mothers present, bucks disperse; mothers absent, fewer disperse. Not only that, but orphaned bucks had higher survival rates, probably because they didn't have to leave their home range. This study then has ramifications for deer management. Remove the mothers via a harvest and you could end up with more bucks on your property. It also suggests that the mothers have something to do with why yearling bucks disperse.

But hold on. Another larger and more recent study done on the eastern shore of Maryland, contradicts this. In this study they observed that bucks orphaned as fawns and non orphaned bucks dispersed at the same rate. (Note, this doesn't mean the above study was wrong, it just means that we got two different results in two different situations.) The Virginia study suggested that female relatives (including the mother) of the yearling buck drive him away, and in so doing reduce the chance for inbreeding. The Maryland study found that the yearling buck-adult doe aggressive interactions were the same for those bucks that dispersed and those that stayed. From this they concluded that dispersal was not caused by maternal aggression as the earlier research showed.

OK, if it isn't the mother driving the young bucks away, what is it? The Maryland data showed that before quality deer management (where higher numbers of adult does are harvested, and small-antlered bucks are not harvested) there was an average per year total of 39 emigrants and 31 immigrants. So 39 left while 31 came in; a net loss of eight yearling bucks per year via dispersal. Researchers believe this is because survival of young bucks living outside the area was low due to heavy hunting pressure, leaving fewer deer available to move into the area. After quality deer management (where hunting pressure is greatly reduced) an average of 26 bucks walked away and 37 bucks moved in, for a net gain of eleven bucks. The gain was attributed to the fact that fewer young bucks dispersed from the area. Researchers observed that 70 percent of yearling bucks walked away from their birth areas before quality deer management, while 55 percent did so after quality deer management.

This is a most interesting finding because those who practice quality deer management are interested in having more bucks on their property. And the fact that fewer yearling bucks disperse after a QDM program is implemented keeps more young bucks on your property.

Before finishing up the results of this Maryland study, let me add some other data on the survival of bucks after implementing a QDM program. One logical question is, *if I protect yearling bucks from harvest, and they do not disperse, will they die from other causes before reaching age 2½?* It's a good question. Dr. Harry Jacobson and his cohorts at Mississippi State University looked at the non-hunting mortality by radio-tracking 238 bucks. They found that natural mortality was low. For example, survivorship for bucks 1½ to 2½ years old was 98 percent (excluding hunting). For bucks 4½ to 5½ it was 87 percent and survival for bucks over 5½ years of age was 80 percent. Thus, there is no worry in Mississippi that the younger bucks you pass up during hunting season will survive till the next year. Most bucks do survive.

However, James Dozier of Clemson University found higher losses in coastal South Carolina. He conducted research on a 7790 acre hunting lease and the objective was to see how many bucks would still be there for the hunters after three years. Forty-seven bucks were followed for the full three years and over that span, thirty bucks died. Non-harvest factors on the site took twelve (14.7%), hunting on the site took seven (14.9%), off-site hunting took another eleven (23.4%). So, hunters on the lease lost the twelve to non-harvest and the eleven that left the area and were shot. What killed the non-harvested deer? Three were eaten by bobcats, three died from disease, two were poached, a car hit one, and three died from unknown causes.

Now back to the reason yearling bucks disperse. The Maryland researchers noted that those bucks that dispersed were involved in more sparring activities with other yearling bucks than those that did not leave their birth places, before and after quality deer management. And they noted less sparring in general after quality deer management. What does this mean?

All young bucks push and shove, and in so doing, they learn who is dominant. However, it's rare for a young buck to spar with an older buck. Thus, the researchers suggested that dispersal is caused by breeding competition between young bucks. That there is less sparring after quality deer management reflects that there are more old bucks around, and the little guys leave these bigger bucks alone. In addition, the presence of older bucks reduces the sparring between the yearling bucks. And it is this lower rate of sparring between yearlings that reduces dispersal rates after quality deer management. There you have it. This is probably the reason that yearling bucks disperse; fighting and sparring with other yearling bucks.

Biologists at the Pennsylvania Cooperative Fish and Wildlife Research Unit also looked at dispersal in two habitats before and after their state-wide antler restriction program. (Note, in essence this is a quality deer management program in that they harvested many more does, and they could not harvest young bucks because of the antler restrictions). Yearling buck dispersal rate was 70 percent in ideal habitat (50% forested), and 44 percent in lesser quality habitat (66% forested). The researchers suggest that when you have more forests, yearling bucks do not disperse as far. During this study increased doe harvests from 2002-2004 lowered overall deer density by 25 percent. The adult doe density decreased by 33 percent, and the sex ratio became more equal. Older bucks (2½-years and older) went up 60 percent. Did this change the rate and timing of dispersal? Not as much as in Maryland, but it did change. Before 2002 they found a 40 percent dispersal in the spring and 30 percent in the fall. After increasing doe harvests and antler restrictions yielding greater numbers of older bucks, they found a decrease in the amount of spring dispersal and an increase in the amount of fall dispersal. Overall, the amount of dispersal had a slight drop.

Though these two studies yielded slightly different results, it appears that if you remove more adult does and protect the young bucks on your property, you get more mature bucks, less fighting among young bucks, and less dispersal. Thus you will have more bucks. Just another reason to harvest more adult does and let young bucks walk.

Here's another question. *Will yearling bucks that live in an area that has low hunting pressure and do not disperse, survive better than those that disperse?* Good question and one 2003 study looked at that. Researchers at the University of Georgia considered ways to reduce the harvest of yearling bucks in order to get more 2½ year-olds in an area. Their approach was simple. Go to a remote 8,400-acre area of West Virginia that has 36 deer per square mile and is heavily hunted. Put a gate up on the only access road forcing hunters to walk into the area. Then put radio collars on yearling deer to see if restricting hunter access reduces harvest.

We know that some yearling bucks leave the area of their birth (disperse), while others do not. The theory behind this study was that bucks that don't emigrate will survive better than those that do, especially since the gate would probably reduce hunter pressure. They radioed 24 yearling bucks; 15 dispersed off the area, and 9 stayed. The average distance of those that moved was 4.4 miles, but one energetic buck traveled 12.8 miles. That's a long way in the rough steep terrain of West Virginia. Eleven of the 15 bucks that left their home area were harvested as yearlings, and 3 more were killed the next fall. Of the nine bucks that stayed on the gated area, four were harvested the first year. Only three lived to their second year and two of those were shot in that second year. So, of the 24 yearlings, only two lived beyond two years of age. The conclusion reached was that locking gates in West Virginia (i.e. reducing hunter access) is not the way to get more yearling bucks to survive and grow.

Next question. *Since many yearling bucks disperse, can you effectively manage all bucks born on one area throughout their life?* Steve Webb and his cohorts at the Caesar Kleberg Wildlife Research Institute in Texas were interested in determining the minimal acreage needed to effectively manage deer. The study was done on a ranch where only mature deer were harvested, and 35% of the bucks on the ranch were at least 5½ years of age. Sounds like a great place to hunt.

As a part of this study, the researchers looked at dispersal and home ranges of various aged bucks. Sixteen of 24 yearlings (67%) dispersed. Thirteen bucks as yearlings had home ranges that were 1,028 acres. Home range sizes for those same bucks at 5½ years of age were 56% smaller at 450 acres. Overlap of these home ranges for bucks as yearlings and at 5½ years was 63%. Mature bucks only move the center of activity of their home ranges by 380 yards per year, indicating little movement from an area once a buck reaches 5½ years of age.

They also found that 15 percent of bucks dispersed after 2½ years of age. One of those bucks dispersed twice before he was 5½ years old. Only 10 percent of all bucks radio collared did not disperse from the time they were 1½ till they were 5½ years of age.

Conclusions

When you consider all the variables that impact deer movement, it tends to boggle the mind. I think that Mickey Hellickson summarized things pretty well when he said that for better hunting success, and understanding the factors that affect deer movement, one should: concentrate your hunting at dawn and dusk, hunt a lot in the rut, stick it out when it rains, and in the northern United States concentrate around the "hunter's" moon.

He also makes one other important yet basic point. Really good bucks probably only make up 5 percent of the deer population, so this makes them hard to hunt. How true that is and that challenge is something hunters have faced since the beginning of time. It is just one of the reasons we love to hunt deer; rain or shine, cold or warm, moon or no moon.

Deer movements retrogress during heavy rain,
but activity remains strong during light showers.

Hunter: *I read the moon theory articles, but get confused with the different moons. From what you've written, it appears that the hunter's moon is the critical one. Right?*

Dave/Bob: *That's right. The hunter's moon is the one tied into the various theories we've written about in this chapter. That is the full moon that usually occurs during the first three weeks of November, but on occasion during the last week of October.*

Hunter: *Let's assume that deer do not feed as much in the daytime when there is a full moon (although you presented some information in this chapter to the contrary). If that is true, then what should be my strategy when I hunt when there is a full moon?*

Dave/Bob: *One thought is to set up in stands as close to the bedding areas as you can get. That will give you the best chance to intercept deer coming and going right at dawn and dusk.*

Hunter: *I see that you noted one well-known hunter-writer who says that when a full moon overlaps the peak of the rut the second and third week of November, it is a good time to hunt. Why is that?*

Dave/Bob: *Dave Morris believes that the full moon intensifies rutting behavior and some of the rutting activity spills over into daylight hours. He goes so far as to say he'd rather hunt the rut when there is a full moon than any other phase of the moon.*

Hunter: *It seems that some older bucks just plain disappear from hunting areas. I know that yearling bucks disperse, but do older bucks also do this?*

Dave/Bob: *Yes, a few older bucks leave their home range for a year, and some then return. There is more on this in Chapter 8. Chapter 10 mentions the fact that individual bucks vary in their behavior. For example, some older bucks do not participate in the rut. They don't mate any does. Same here. Some older bucks move around a lot, some even leave their home range for* *awhile, but others stay put. These kinds of data are starting to show us that there is a lot of individual variation in older bucks. This makes it harder to predict movements, or locations, and obviously makes it harder to hunt certain bucks. But, it also makes the challenge more intense, and the hunt all the more rewarding.*

Hunter: *You covered a number of studies on the moon's impact on the initiation of the rut and rutting movements. In some cases one study contradicts another, so what is the best hunting strategy?*

Dave/Bob: *Our first suggestion is quite simple and straight forward. Hunt a lot in the rut. From the last week of October to Thanksgiving, if you live in the northern half of the country, you should be bowhunting and/or gun hunting. Also, concentrate your hunting at dawn and dusk. Also in the North, spend even more time hunting the week after, and even during, the hunter's moon. Relative to some other data we presented in this chapter, stick it out when it rains. There are many variables that affect a deer's movement, and they don't always work together at the same time. Thus, there is lots of variation relative to deer and buck movement.*

Hunter: *I understand that as many as 70 percent of yearling bucks disperse, and that the probable reason is that they fight with other young bucks, meaning the cause is buck competition. Then you presented data showing that with a quality deer management program, fewer yearling bucks will disperse. It was suggested that part of the reason that fewer yearlings left the area was because there is less hunting pressure on private leases that practice quality deer management. Finally, it was noted that one of the effects of dispersal is that inbreeding with family members will be greatly reduced as young bucks move to new areas to live.*
So, if I have a really nice piece of deer habitat, well managed, and I practice a quality deer management program, do I really want to hold more yearling bucks on my property if it will lead to inbreeding?

Dave/Bob: *What a great question. Remember, when you practice quality deer management, you end up with more, older bucks. And older, mature bucks will do at least seventy percent of the breeding of does (see chapter 10). But, if those older bucks were born on your area and did not disperse, then they could be breeding with their own mothers, sisters, and* daughters. However, even when there is quality deer management, you get some dispersal. Inbreeding would not occur over night. It would take many years for the negative impacts of inbreeding to show up. Our guess is that if thirty percent of your yearling bucks leave, and some new bucks come in, you probably will never see any impacts from inbreeding. The reason is that even though your mature bucks will do seventy percent of the breeding, each buck will only mate 3-4 does, and many will only mate one. This factor will reduce the chances of much inbreeding.

Hunter: *My hunting buddy feels that bucks move around more the two weeks prior to the peak of the rut, but I believe they move more during the peak rut when they are with does. Are there data on this?*

Dave/Bob: *Yes there are data. A study done on the McAlester Army Ammunition Plant in Oklahoma looked at buck movements before, during and after the rut. Age is definitely a variable relative to buck movements at this time. Between October 1 and December 15, bucks over 5½ years of age traveled the furthest, followed by movements of bucks 3½ and 4½ years of age. Maximum distances traveled by bucks 1½ and 2½ years of age was probably ⅓ that of older bucks. During the rut, not only did older bucks travel further during the rut, but also they did it faster than younger bucks. Young bucks tended to walk in a straight line from one location to another, while older bucks moved all over, and they were in a hurry as they went. What is happening is the oldest bucks rove all over looking for females, then they chase them around. Though some of the younger bucks will mate does, most don't so they don't move around all that much. To summarize, in the pre rut yearling bucks move a fair amount; in the rut their movements are reduced; in the post rut, yearling bucks move the least. For the mature bucks, they move much more than other bucks during the peak of the rut.*

One other thing the authors of this study pointed out. When looking at the complexity of the paths taken by bucks, in good habitat, buck movement paths were high in complexity. This is caused by bucks moving quickly from one source of good habitat (where there might be does) to another location with good habitat. The females are predictably found where there is good food or thick secure cover and the bucks go there.

The once believed theory that the majority of does were bred by older bucks with the largest racks is not true.

CHAPTER 10

Breeding Data That May Surprise You

ere was the scenario. I was hunting my prize area in Ohio on a cold November 3rd morning. Rut sign was everywhere and it was just one of those times when you knew something was about to happen. I picked up my rattling horns, but paused because of rustling in the leaves.

Rustling is an understatement. Deer were running and headed my way. I quickly dropped the antlers, and grabbed the bow. A doe came crashing by, with a small buck hot on her tail. One minute later a small six point came trailing by, following the path of the others. Then a second doe ran down the trail, hotly followed by a decent eight pointer. Twenty seconds later another, bigger, buck followed, and right behind him was a bruiser.

All these deer were headed out into a new clear-cut, and in my mind I felt there were two hot does, plus at least five bucks. They all ran out of sight, but shortly thereafter here comes one of the does, with the biggest buck right on her tail. She looked exhausted and I figured he'd been on her all night. Eighty yards out he mounted her; this is what the rut is all about.

Then off to my left, along the edge of the clear-cut, I spotted the smallest buck and he too was mating a doe. With two bigger bucks in the area, that surprised me. Then again, one of the big guys was busy, so he obviously couldn't be mating the other doe. I never did find out what happened to the other bigger buck. All I know is that after the mating, the little buck followed the hot doe right under my stand while the big guy moved away with the second hot doe. No shots, but what an exciting morning.

This scenario is played out hundreds of thousands of times each year. Bucks mating does. I grew up believing that only the biggest, most dominant bucks, mated does. In fact, I'll bet that most of you reading this right now believe that older bucks do almost all of the mating and the bigger antlered guys breed many does. Turns out, that isn't always the case.

Twins may be the product of two separate sires.

Do big bucks do all the breeding?

We once believed that breeding was done by just a few older, dominant bucks. Today we know that breeding is distributed among a large number of bucks of all ages. What follows is a summary of some studies that prove this fact. In these studies, researchers used DNA tests as the basis for determining what bucks breed does. The first study was done in Texas and it answered two age-old questions; do older bucks (as compared to younger bucks) play a major role in mating does? And, does antler size have anything to do with reproductive success? The study was cleverly designed.

Bucks were captured in the wild and categorizes as; high quality bucks scoring over 120 inches, low quality bucks scoring less than 90 inches, young bucks that were 1½ years of age, and older bucks that were 4½ years of age or older. These bucks, from all categories, along with some wild-captured does, were placed in two 500-acre pens. All deer were tagged and DNA samples taken so that the parents of all offspring could be identified.

The first finding answered a question that no one had even suspected before DNA technology — *do sets of twin fawns have the same father?* Based on this study, and others we'll mention, the answer is "no." Twin fawns sometimes have different fathers. In this study, 8 of 37 sets of twin fawns had different fathers. We've always believed that when you saw a doe with twin fawns, they were identical twins; meaning they had one father. However, in the past four years, several studies have been done where they used DNA tests on fawns to determine the parents. Basically it works the same as Crime Stopper on television. Wildlife researchers sampled the DNA of as many does and bucks in an area, then the next spring they sample the DNA of as many fawns as possible. One study was the one we are discussion and was conducted in two 5,000-acre pens in Texas. The second was done in the wild on a wildlife management area in Oklahoma and the third in a 1280-acre pen in Michigan.

This particular buck showed up on a South Texas ranch with a sex ratio
slightly favoring males in the post rut period without a broken tine,
perhaps indicating that he did not participate in the rut.

In all three cases, between 20-25 percent of twin fawns had different fathers. We've all seen a hot doe being harassed and chased by more than one buck. Anna Bess conducted the Michigan study and theorized that non-identical twin fawns were conceived in this manner. A younger buck finds a hot doe and mates her. Then a dominant older buck moves in and drives the younger guy away, and mates the doe. Bess's data support this theory because in the six set of twins that she found with different fathers, in every case one of the fathers was 2½ to 5½ years of age, while the second buck was either 5½ or 6½ years of age.

The fact that you now know that about one-quarter of all twin fawns have different fathers won't help your hunting success, but there's obviously more to hunting than harvesting. Aldo Leopold once said that the more we know about something, the more we appreciate it. True for deer.

What about our expectations that older bucks mate more does than yearling bucks? In the Texas pen study, they did. In fact, in one of the two 5,000-acre pens, 44 percent of all bucks were yearlings and they did 4 percent of the mating. In the second pen yearlings comprised 32 percent of the bucks and did 7 percent of the mating. Even in a large pen, where the little bucks can't hide from bigger bucks, some of the yearlings mated does.

Which older bucks in the pens did the most mating? Here the results were a bit of a surprise. In the first pen, a 7½ year-old buck bred only two does. But a pitiful 5½ year-old buck that weighed only 78 pounds and had an 11-inch spread, bred six does. Apparently attitude matters. In the second pen the best breeder was a 5½ year-old buck that bred 16 does. But the biggest buck (4½ years old and scoring 146 inches) only bred one doe. In one of those pens, one ten point buck that scored 150 inches didn't mate at all; nor did a 4-year-old buck that had low quality horns. Yes, apparently attitude matters.

Note however, that quite a few low quality bucks did mate, and one mediocre buck in particular mated a lot. That buck only had a rack scoring 126 inches, but he mated 16 of 26 does in one pen.

Thus, when it comes to mating bucks, things aren't what they seem. The researchers concluded that the reproductive system in white-tailed deer is more complex than we once thought. Indeed we have to ask why a few older, large bucks don't participate in mating, while at the same time younger bucks are doing some of the mating. The researchers also concluded that because some inferior older bucks mated more does than superior older bucks, some individuals have attitude. Some more, some less. Obviously that 126-inch buck had attitude.

Some aggressive bucks regardless of age or rack size, breed more doe than others,
but on average, most bucks only mate successfully with
one to three does on an annual basis.

OK, we know that in pens yearlings do some of the mating, but what about in the wild? There are data, and they too confirm that in the wild, under different buck to doe sex ratios, and under different age structures, some young bucks mate does. Dr. Randy DeYoung has some data collected on a 3,000-acre fenced area in SW Oklahoma that also shows that even when you have a lot of older bucks in an area, some young bucks mate does. Dr. DeYoung had DNA from 40-60 percent of all deer (502 deer, 300 fawns) in the area over an 8-year period. He then was able to match the DNA of the fawns to that of bucks, and learned which buck sired which fawn. No surprise that older bucks sired most fawns. Only 30 percent of the bucks in the population were 3½ years old or older, but they sired 65

Yearling bucks can sneak in and breed hot does during the peak of the rut when mature bucks are tending other does.

percent of the fawns. Twenty-six percent were 2½ and they sired 21 percent of the fawns. Forty-four percent of the bucks were 1½ year olds and they only sired 14 percent of the fawns (see Table 1). But the point is that those yearlings did mate does.

Table 1.

Percent of bucks in each age class and the percent of does sired in Oklahoma and Texas.

	Bucks 1½ yrs old (does sired)	2½ yrs old (does sired)	3½ yrs old+ (does sired)
OK	44% (14%)	26% (21%)	30% (65%)
TX	23% (14%)	19% (16%)	57% (70%)

DeYoung also collected data that answers the question, *how many does will one buck mate in a breeding season?* I grew up believing that the average buck mated 6-8 does each year. Had I given that some thought, I'd have realized that such was highly improbable. A doe stays in heat for two-three days and a buck will stay with her for that time. A majority of does will be bred in a two week period, maybe less, so an individual buck will have difficulty mating many does in a season.

This DNA study answered the question and confirms that indeed, it is difficult for bucks to mate many does. In fact, on average, *most bucks only mated successfully with one doe.* However, one 4½ year-old buck sired fawns from six does. Also on this area, over their entire life span, 61 bucks sired 154 fawns, but only one buck sired more than five fawns in one year. In fact, only five bucks sired three fawns in two successive years. He also found that only 30 percent of does raised twins successfully and only 22 percent of all does raised twins successfully two years in a row; only 3 percent did so three years in a row. Age was definitely a factor as

86 percent of fawns born to does over 3½ years of age lived beyond six months.

DeYoung also looked at the age of bucks that breed on a wildlife management area in Mississippi where buck harvest is high (yielding a lot of yearling bucks in the population) and the sex ratio is seven does per buck. This scenario is common to many northern and eastern states where hunters take a high percentage of all yearling bucks alive each year, and there are lots of does per buck. On his Mississippi wildlife management area, 64 percent of the bucks were 1½ years old, 17 percent were 2½ and 11 percent were 3½. The data show that 70 percent of the breeding was done by mature bucks, while 30 percent was done by yearlings.

Finally, he looked at bucks on the King Ranch in Texas, which is heavily managed for older bucks. There, only 23 percent of the bucks were 1½ years of age, and they sired 14 percent of all fawns (See Table 1). Nineteen percent of the bucks were 2½ and they sired 16 percent of all fawns; 57 percent of bucks were 3½ years of age or older and they sired 70 percent of all fawns.

Thus, DeYoung had data from three different areas; one (Mississippi) where the males are heavily exploited and there were lots of does per buck and lots of yearlings; a trophy management ranch (Texas) where only fully mature bucks were harvested and there were 2.7 does per buck; and a quality deer management area (Oklahoma) with 44 percent yearling bucks and 30 percent old, mature bucks. In all three areas, yearlings sired some does.

Why don't mature bucks do all the mating?

Probably because they can't. Dr. DeYoung points out that elk and deer are different. Elk bulls have harems and they keep pretty tight control over all the cows in their group. They fight and defend those cows. Deer are not a harem species. They do not round up and control herds of does. They find a hot doe and tend her until mating. They may mate that one doe several times, even as many as eight times.* In the two-three days that this is going on, other bucks in the area are mating hot does. While the mature buck is busy, a younger buck may mate a doe, close beside that mature buck. That is the reality of the deer's mating system.

If mature bucks do a lot of the breeding, can we get inbreeding in an area?

That used to be a concern since it was believed that one to two mature bucks did the breeding in an area. However, one recent study showed that big bucks don't stay on top more than one year. If a buck is the dominant buck in an area, his reign usually lasts only one year before another big buck displaces him. In fact, a pen study done in Mississippi showed several instances during the rut where a dominant 6-year-old buck was replaced by a 3½ year old.

Also consider the DeYoung data for the three sites. On the Mississippi site, 16 bucks sired 20 fawns. On the Texas ranch, 70 fawns were sired by 46 bucks, and on the Oklahoma wildlife management area, 61 bucks sired 154 fawns. While it is true that some older bucks sire more than one fawn (in fact some 3½ year-old bucks and 4½ year-old bucks sire three or four fawns a year), with all the data showing that a variety of bucks do the mating, inbreeding is not a problem. This next study also shows that many different aged bucks mate does.

In a 1,280-acre pen in Michigan, where the sex ratio was 1.5 does per buck, we find that older bucks do most mating, but some yearlings do as well (Table 2). Only 3 of 16 yearling bucks bred does while 11 of 13 bucks over 4½ year of age, bred does. Of all bucks over 4½ years of age, a 4½ year old was the most successful breeder; he bred seven does.

*Not every mating yields a fawn. About 20 percent of the times bucks mount does, no fawns are produced.

Table 2.

The number of bucks in each age class and the number of those bucks that bred does, in a 1,280-acre pen in Michigan.

Age Class	1½	2½	3½	4½	5½	6½+
Bucks in Age Class	16	4	1	6	4	3
Bucks Breeding In Each Age Class	3	2	1	5	4	2

Remember though, this is in a pen. Note that one of oldest bucks in the pen did not breed any does. We've said it before; attitude does matter.

Inbreeding will not be a factor because lots of different bucks mate does, and the best yearlings breed some does as well. In areas where lots of young bucks are harvested, with fewer older age classed bucks, some young bucks do the mating. In areas managed for older age classes, older bucks do a higher percentage of the breeding compared to yearling bucks. Even so, we see that in all three of the areas DeYoung studied, areas with lots of does and young bucks and areas with lots of older bucks, yearling bucks still mate some does.

In summary, yearling bucks mate some does, but older bucks do the most mating. Also, the average buck only mates one doe per year, but older bucks may mate three or four. Obviously, dominance is important, but if the older bucks are busy chasing does, than a yearling can step in and be successful. A good rule of thumb is that yearling bucks sire around 30 percent of all fawns.

Hunter: *I live in one of those states you mentioned, where hunters take 80 percent of all the live yearling bucks every year. We have lots of does, and few mature bucks. This means that I have very little chance of taking a good buck. What are the negatives of all this, and what can I do about it?*

Dave/Bob: *You are not alone as this is typical in parts of many states, especially in the East. No doubt many yearling bucks are mating does. However, the yearlings that are doing the mating are probably the best yearlings. There is no data to support this, but it makes sense that the strongest, most fit, yearlings would be doing much of the breeding. Of course you do have some older bucks there, and they definitely breed does too.*

Now to the question, what can I do about this situation, and what can I do to get an opportunity to shoot larger bucks? As an individual, on the state level, the best you can do is voice your interest in adopting a management program that will get the sex ratio somewhere close to normal. This will be difficult, not so much because the state wildlife agency is not supportive, but hunters will not be supportive. You see, once you start knocking down the does, hunters will complain. A better way to get a management system started that will increase buck age structure is to do it on your own lease, or your own property. Once you are successful, then your neighbors will be coming to you asking how you did it? From there it will spread. It happens all the time.

Hunter: *One subject you didn't cover is how to determine how many breeding bucks I have on my property. I've been doing spotlight counts every August, running the same route three evenings in a row. I use this to determine my buck to doe ratio and that helps me determine how many adult does I need to harvest each year. Of course my goal is to eliminate the does I don't need and leave more of that food the does would eat for the bucks. But, is this technique the best to determine the number of bucks out there?*

Dave/Bob: *That is a great question. There is one study recently done by Mickey Hellickson that showed that using trail cameras put at selected locations, allowed them to identify many more individual bucks than they saw during spotlight surveys. They suggest you use one camera for every 100 acres. Now you can buy enough cameras to cover your property, or you can rotate cameras from one location to the next. Pick the best spots you think bucks will walk and the cameras will photograph lots of bucks. However, another study shows that the older the buck, the less likely they will be photographed, probably because their home range gets smaller as they age.*

Rubs are signposts for deer and hunters. Size of rack as well as direction the buck travels can often be determined by analyzing a rub or series of them.

CHAPTER 11

Here's The Rub;
Your Key to
Better Hunting

The material in the next two chapters is what triggered us to write this book. We listened to researchers and read their papers on all the new work they were doing on rubs and scrapes and decided that a book that summarized this type of information was needed. We believe that what you find here will be fascinating and helpful as you attempt to learn more about whitetails. As with some of the other chapters, we'll present it in a question and answer format, as that seems to be a good way to convey the most information in an organized fashion.

Before getting to the questions, let's talk a minute about how bucks rub a tree. A buck will approach the sapling or tree, pushing their antlers up and down as they rub. They will pause for short periods and sniff and lick the part of the tree just rubbed. Now to why they rub.

Why do bucks rub trees?

When we were kids growing up in Pennsylvania, our dads taught us that rubs are made by bucks trying to remove the velvet. Of course later we'd notice that (1) the velvet was gone by early September, and (2) most rubs were made in October. Obviously bucks rub trees as they remove velvet, but it really doesn't explain most rubbing.

Rubs are "signposts" and as such they have several functions. Gene and Barry Wensel, two of the most observant and perceptive deer hunters that ever took to the woods, believe that bucks see rubs, use them as visual cues, as they walk trails. Using that knowledge they have been able to "move deer trails" as much as 20-30 yards simply by "moving the rub line." There are hunting situations where you want to hunt a rub line, but either there are no trees where you need them for a stand, or the wind just isn't right. The Wensel brothers make a series of new rubs, taking off from the original rub line, and the bucks will follow those rubs... right past your tree stand. Neat huh?

However, note one thing. The Wensel's do not hunt rub lines per se. Their stands may at times be near a rub line, but they select the location for tree stands based on terrain and structure. In their scouting, they look at the big picture, look for pinch sites that funnel deer, and look for structure in the habitat that leads deer to walk in a certain direction and path. They focus on habitat edges; small, subtle saddles; thick ground cover that forces deer to move around it; etc. Sometimes that area may contain rub lines, sometimes that area may lead to rub lines, but they do not selectively pick out a rub line and set up a tree stand. For more on how they do what they do, go to www.brothersofthebow.com.

Now back to the rubs. Not only are rubs visual signpost, they are chemical signposts. With the advent of cameras being placed at rubs, we now know that bucks rub more than their antlers. They also rub their forehead gland on trees and leave chemical messages there for others to smell. Drs. Larry Marchinton and Karl Miller have conducted much research on signposts in their deer research pens at the University of Georgia. They suggest that when a mature buck rubs a tree, the odors send messages to other bucks and does. These odors play a role in the timing of estrus, and in suppressing aggressive behavior by younger bucks.

Are there different kinds of rubs?

Yes indeed. Let's eliminate the meaningless ones first. As you walk along the edge of a field you often find a number of very small rubs, randomly occurring, always on small saplings. For the most part these are rubs made by yearling bucks and are inconsequential. The bucks just walk along a trail, come to an intersection, smell some doe odor and make a rub. All it tells you is that a little buck walked by. He may return, he may never return.

The rubs that really mean something are large rubs found each year on the same tree. Dr. Grant Woods conducted the first major study of these

Traditional rubs, particularly large ones, used over a long period of time, have been considered big buck magnets.

"traditional" rubs on the Bluff Plantation in South Carolina. He defined "traditional" rubs as those used for more than three years. He camera monitored nine traditional rubs and found bucks with eight or more points touched or rubbed the tree when visiting 50 percent of the time while spikes only rubbed or touched the tree 27 percent of the time they visited the traditional rubs. Obviously bigger bucks have more interest in traditional rubs. Interestingly, in 33 percent of the photos taken of does at the rubs, they rubbed their body against the tree. Bucks never did that.

It would be sheer speculation to determine the meaning of all the behaviors that go on at traditional rubs, but it is certain that they are a focal area for communication between dominant bucks and lesser bucks, and between bucks and does.

Table 1.

Buck behaviors Dr. Woods recorded on photographs at nine traditional rubs, 1991-1992.

Antler touches tree	54%
Smells tree	50%
Antlers rub tree	31%
Forehead touches tree	12%
Butt touches tree	8%

Dr. Woods found that more than one mature buck used most traditional rubs, and at one of his rubs he photographed thirteen different mature bucks in one month and four of those bucks used that rub in successive years. Yep, traditional rubs are spots you might like to hunt. But here's the rub (sorry, we just couldn't help ourselves). Although bucks visited these rubs during the rut, almost all did so at night. Does this mean you should abandon such sites as you make plans for this year's hunting? Absolutely not. Do some preseason scouting and look for large trees that were rubbed the previous year. Concentrate on them this fall. Remember traditional rubs are made and kept active by several rather sizable bucks. Look for feeding areas near the rubs. Look for scrape lines. Just because most bucks visit the traditional rubs at night does not mean they don't pass through that area during hunting hours.

In our experience traditional rubs are much more productive when you have a deer herd with a balanced sex ratio—say, one buck to one, two or three does. With any more does than that, such sites do not seem to be used as much. Perhaps having many does in heat walking around an area makes scent communication to bucks much easier, thus eliminating the need for the rubs.

Table 2.

Deer activity near traditional rubs based on photographs taken.* **

% buck photos taken 9 PM-6 AM	74%
% buck photos taken 9 PM-3 AM	48%
% buck photos taken 6 PM-9 PM	24%
% doe photos taken 9 PM-6 AM	60%
% fawn photos taken 9 PM-6 AM	51%

* Buck activity near traditional rubs increased a lot during the breeding season, but the percentage of day vs. night photographs did not change during the study even though there was increased gun hunting pressure (some of it near traditional rubs) during the hunting season.

** From 379 photographs taken, only twice was the same buck photographed twice at the same rub in one 24-hour period.

When do bucks rub?

After the velvet is shed, the rubs that really mean something start appearing in September in most whitetail country. Though there is little data to support this, most experts believe that the mature bucks will make a few big rubs in September, so when you find these, you are on to something. Noted deer hunter, and good bowhunting friend, Steve Bartylla, believes that although large-antlered bucks usually rub big trees, these early September rubs may be found on brush and "unimpressive tree trunks." He goes on to explain that in order to determine if a rub is made by a big buck, check out the collateral damage. Small bucks just make neat little rubs. But big bucks tear things up. If they rub a shrub, it will be all torn up. If they rub small saplings, they will break them off, and tear several up at one time.

Young bucks start rubbing in most of whitetail country in October. Most of the small rubs that pop up in mid to late October are made by yearling bucks for the most part, and mean very little. When you find an explosion of small rubs in October, they often are the result of the dispersing yearling bucks that just arrived in your hunting territory. These yearling bucks make a rub, a nice simple rub, and move on. The bigger guys get into it. They are over aggressive, feeling their hormones and have prior experience in making rubs. They will push, shove, break and tear. They will sometimes leave scars on the trees from their brow tines. Sometimes you can determine the spread of such bucks as the tips may touch nearby trees.

Older bucks usually make the traditional rubs, but don't always look like they've been hammered. You may just see a light rubbing on such trees, but make no mistake about it; traditionally rubbed trees are focal centers for

Although young bucks make scrapes, larger bucks exert more aggression when making a scrape, making them easier to identify because of all the collateral damage.

big buck communication. Dr. Grant Woods' camera monitored traditional rubs and found that buck visits were highest in October, and next highest in November in South Carolina. Peak use of traditional rubs was the last two weeks of October.

Where do bucks rub?

Part of where bucks rub will be determined by what they rub. Do bucks prefer certain species of trees? In some areas the answer is a definite "yes." The first published data on this topic is found in a 1974 scientific paper titled, "Marking behavior and its social function in white-tailed deer," by W. G. Moore and R. L. Marchinton. They found that aromatic tree species were rubbed quite often in southern Georgia. Kile and Marchinton published a follow-up study on tree species used as rubs in a 1977 issue of The American Midland Naturalist. They also found that aromatic species were rubbed more than other species. In this case the species most rubbed were black cherry and Eastern juniper.

Dr. Grant Woods followed this with a detailed look at rubbed tree species on a site in South Carolina. Although he found rubs on 22 species of trees, traditional rubs were made on only 11 species. Even more informative was the fact that of all the traditional rubs, half were found on aromatic species of trees... Eastern red cedar, Southern magnolia, and sassafras. That confirmed what I (DS) had found on my Ohio hunting sites where traditional rubs were almost always made on red cedar trees.

Do bucks rub on these species because there are lots of such trees out there? No. Dr. Wood found that the three aromatic species rubbed made up only four percent of all trees growing on his study sites. Clearly bucks seek these tree species for traditional rubs. When Wood looked at smaller non-traditional rubs, again he found that bucks preferred aromatic tree species, even though they made up only a small percentage of trees in the forest. So, at least in this study area, smaller bucks also prefer aromatic trees to rub.

Table 3.

Traditional rubs made on aromatic specie tend to be used in successive years. Here is data from the five traditional trees that were antler rubbed in 1990 and in 1991, and the four traditional rubs not antler rubbed in both years.

Traditional rubs; tree species used in both years.	3 sassafras, 1 cedar, 1 magnolia
Non-traditional rubs; tree species not used in both years.	1 red maple, 1 laurel oak, 1 chinaberry, 1 magnolia

The three most used aromatic species have yellow- or orange-colored wood that is soft, light and close-grained. We're not sure why bucks would rub such species year after year. Perhaps such trees are oily and hold the forehead gland odor more than other trees. In fact, Woods found hair on 38 percent of the 115 rubs he found in a Missouri study indicating that they rub their forehead gland. In that study the top rubbed tree species were cedar (31), dogwood (28), serviceberry (15), and hickory (13). Interestingly only one sassafras was rubbed, but this was predominantly a scrape study so no data were presented on the amount of sassafras in the area. There may have been little.

Dr. Karl Miller and his cohorts published an antler rub study in a 1987 issue of the Journal of Wildlife Management. They looked at rubs on five Georgia wildlife management areas and found that deer rubbed 47 of 58 available tree species. In other words, they rubbed just about every species out there. The highest percentage of rubs occurred on the three species that were most abundant on the areas; red maple (16 percent of rubs), flowering dogwood (12 percent of rubs) and Virginia pine (10 percent of rubs). Species that were rubbed in amounts that exceeded their availability were alders, cherries, Virginia pine, Eastern juniper, white pine, common witch

Because of the deer's dependence on water in Texas, retama, one of the predominant trees in the riparian zone, are often targeted by bucks.

hazel, and striped maple. The researchers did not discuss aromatic species and we do not know if many were on the study sites.

From the above list, Eastern juniper, and witch hazel would probably be considered aromatic. However, they noted that blackgum tupelo and American sweetgum, both of which would be aromatic, were rubbed less commonly than available. So at least in this area it does not seem that aromatic species were rubbed as often as in other areas. The authors also did not separate out traditional from non traditional rubs and that might explain the results.

Bryan Kinkel conducted a thorough case study on a ridge and valley site in Tennessee where he was able to correlate topography with the occurrence of rubs. He found the highest density of rubs per acre (eight) in the first 10 meters from an edge. When he got more than 20 meters from an edge he found only three rubs per acre. He also found a lot of rubs along ridge tops and saddles on ridges.

Kinkel then went on to examine various types of edges. He found that the highest density of rubs (20 per acre) were within 10 meters of a soft edge. Hard edges had twelve rubs per acre and road edges ten. A soft edge is where mature forests meet younger growth, whereas a hard edge is one where forests meet fields or along a power line right of way. In South Texas, Zaiglin observed the highest percentage of rub activity along the riparian zone. This he attributed to the importance of water in the semi arid brush country.

What determines the amount of rubbing?

Several studies state that yearling bucks make only half of the rubs that mature bucks make. Obviously then mature bucks, big bucks, make a lot of rubs. Dr. Karl Miller and cohorts at the University of Georgia looked at rubbing on five wildlife management areas in northern Georgia and found an average of 500 to 1,500 rubs per square mile. They also found that an average buck will make between 69 and 538 rubs a year. Interestingly, the 69 rubs/buck were found on the wildlife management area with a high buck density, while the 538 rubs/ buck were from a low buck density. The researchers also noted that a buck makes around 15-20 rubs a day during the pre rut and rut. Now here is the kicker. They concluded that rub density was correlated with the number of bucks 2½-years old and older (see Table 4). This might explain why the lowest amount of rubs/buck was found on the wildlife area with the highest buck density. The area with the high buck density may not have had many older bucks, while the area with low buck density probably had a proportionately high number of older bucks.

Table 4.

The relation of the number of rubs to the density of older bucks on five wildlife management areas in northern Georgia, 1982-83.

	# 2.5 yr-old bucks/sq. km.	# rubs/sq. km.
Lake Russell WMA	1.0	425
Cohutta WMA	0.9	432
Berry College WMA	0.6	310
Coosawattee WMA	0.5	286
Chestattee WMA	0.5	330

Miller also found that mast affects the amount of rubbing. During the second year of their study, two of the wildlife management areas had fair mast, but on the remaining three areas there was a mast failure. Note that northern Georgia, where this study was done, is only fair deer habitat with little agriculture. Thus, deer rely on mast. When the mast failed, rub density plummeted. The authors believe that deer had to spend more time foraging for food, and this decreased time for rubbing. They also noted that

November body weights of older bucks decreased by 4.3 percent on the three wildlife area that had no acorns. On the two areas that had acorns, older buck weights increased by 4.5 percent. The researchers suggest that the intensity of the rut may have been decreased in response to their poorer body condition, leading to fewer rubs.

How does all this information help me?

When we were younger, actually much younger, in the early bow season you'd find us sitting near the edge of a food plot or agricultural field. In a few weeks there would be a lot of rubs in that area, again confirming the selection of a great spot to bowhunt. Problem was, with some hunting pressure in the area, we never got a shot at a good buck in those situations. Actually it would be rare to see a good buck in those situations.

Although traditional rubs are used more often by mature bucks, many of these visits are conducted under the security of darkness.

Finding rubs in September will be a clue to what is out there. Come October, find a rub line, and find one that has been used for several years. If you can find an aromatic tree on that line that has been rubbed for several years, all the better, because such traditional rubs usually attract several really good bucks.

We know that mature bucks do most of their rubbing at night. In fact, as we saw in chapter 9, except for the peak rut, bucks do most of their moving around at night. But if you find a hot rub line, along a ridge top, leading to and from a good food source, and you've seen lots of smaller bucks using that area, stick with it. Come the pre rut, just before the main rut, there is a chance that a good buck will walk by you. Same for acorns. When you find a good white oak that is dropping acorns and there is feeding sign there, find the rub line leading to that food source. And if you can find a traditional rub on that line, again, you've got the spot.

We love to hunt funnels. When you have a mix of dense hardwoods and agricultural fields, finding a funnel, a narrow strip of cover leading into a field, or between a field, or at the bottom of a ridge, is a super place to set up. Often a rub line will lead to and from a funnel, and when the big boys get active, you need to be there.

John Ozoga is one the leading research experts on whitetail deer. For years he collected data on an enclosed herd in the Upper Peninsula of Michigan. Earlier we mentioned the way the Wensel brothers were able to move a deer trail, by making rubs on trees. John did something a bit different in his large deer pen. He placed a number of trembling aspen poles in the ground. The poles were roughly two inches in diameter and six feet tall. He found that deer in his pen rubbed these poles a great deal. However, there are no studies where artificial poles have ever been rubbed in the wild. We're not sure that this information will help your hunting. Putting poles in the ground might result in some bucks rubbing them, but we doubt that they will impact your success. However, making rubs on trees along trails will get noticed by bucks. And making those rubs off of the trail, in order to move that trail closer to your stand, has been done. In certain situations, that approach can work.

Rub lines and traditional rubs are real clues to where bucks travel, where good bucks travel. Find those and you enhance your chance of seeing a good buck.

Hunter: *OK guys, let me try to make some sense from all this science and apply it to where I hunt. It sounds like most rubs don't mean much. Little bucks just stop at deer path intersections or walk along edges and when they smell any doe urine, or just whenever their own hormones kick in, they make rubs. Lots of rubs. Doesn't seem that this helps me at all.*

Bob/Dave: *Maybe that is partly right, but let's not throw the baby out with the bath water. First, lots of rubs tell you that there are a fair number of bucks in the area, regardless of age. Ignore most of those little rubs scattered all over. Focus on traditional rubs on aromatic trees. Rubs that are there year after year. Such rubs tell you that mature bucks are using the area and coming to those trees.*

Hunter: *Fine, but you said that most of the time they come to such traditional rubs at night?*

Bob/Dave: *That is true, but even so, finding such rubs tells you several things. First, there are some big bucks in the area. And since more than one mature buck may visit a traditional rub, you may be looking at several good bucks in your area. Second, if you know they are rubbing a traditional rub, then back track, using aerial photos, or maps, as well as on-the-ground investigations and try to determine where they feed and bed. That traditional rub is located somewhere in between and finding that rub may well help you to determine where to place some stands. And don't forget that 24 percent of the time bucks visit these traditional rubs in the day time, probably early morning. Thus, hunting near them can also put you in a place for success.*

Hunter: *I hunt an area that doesn't have many rubs. Does that mean I don't have many bucks, or many deer in the area?*

Bob/Dave: *Obviously that could mean there are few deer in the area. But studies show that where you have lots of does you get less rubbing and where you have a good doe to buck sex ratio, you get fewer rubs. And a good doe to buck ratio, say 3 to 1 or 2 to 1 is a good thing. Those kind or ratios usually mean good bucks in the area. When you have those kind of ratios you should also find fewer rubs, but good, big rubs on trees, because there are more mature bucks in the area.*

Hunter: *Any last suggestions on things that will help me?*

Bob/Dave: *Don't forget, as we mentioned above, rub lines and funnels are important. Funnels near traditional rubs may be a great spot for a stand. And rubs may also tie into scrapes, as we will discuss in the next chapter. Hunting big bucks is a never-ending puzzle. You learn one thing, but in so doing discover two other mysteries that need solved. The challenge never ends, making your whitetail hunting a continuing saga that will never end.*

Located above most if not all scrapes will be an overhanging limb upon which a deer rubs its preorbital and forehead glands.

CHAPTER 12

The Latest Dirt
on Scrapes

N o matter how long you have deer hunted, we dare you to walk
past a scrape without checking it out. How fresh is it? How
big is it? Was it there last year? Did he tear up the overhanging
branches? Is there a track in the scrape? Where are the entrance and exit
routes? Every scrape is a story, a mystery, something that tweaks at the
hunter within.

We are no different than the average hunter, because we also are
intrigued by scrapes. We, like many of you, believed for years that a
dominant buck would make a scrape and estrous does would visit it. If a
lesser buck came near, he steered clear of the scrape. Then the big buck
would come back periodically, wind check the scrape, and if a hot doe had
been there, he'd pick up her scent and catch up to her. Then the chase was
on. It all made sense (sorry, a little play on words, scents), but new studies
on scrapes done in recent years gives us a different perspective on what
happens there.

Scrapes have long been defined as a pawed area in the soil 3-4 feet beneath an overhanging branch. The first major scrape study was published in 1987 by Dr. Karl Miller and was based on work done on a penned deer herd at the University of Georgia. In those pens scraping was related to buck age (only mature dominant bucks did most of the scraping), testosterone level, and hierarchical position in the herd. They also found that sub-ordinate bucks can mark and lick the overhanging limb, but they rarely interact with the scrape itself (i.e. paw, urinate). Remember though, this was a pen study and we will learn that there can be biases associated with such studies. For example, being in a pen, the deer can't really move as much as they might in the wild. Also, the deer were only observed during the day. Still, this research was valuable and well done.

In the years after the Miller study we still did not know a whole lot about scrapes, who used them, when, etc., until the advent of remote-sensing cameras. Cameras opened up a whole new world, not only for hunters, but also for researchers interested in the meaning of scrapes. And video cameras with night lighting opened up things even more. Do only the dominant bucks visit scrapes? When do they visit? What behaviors occur when bucks (and does) come to scrapes? These are just some of the questions that we will examine as we consider the latest dirt on scrapes.

Why do bucks make scrapes?

Scrapes are like rubs, signposts that have to do with olfactory and/or visual communication and to a lesser degree, with dominance in bucks. The Miller study mentioned above, and other research, showed that scrapes are places where does let bucks know whether they are ready to breed. Scrapes also probably tell members of the opposite sex that they were there. Bottom line, we've always believed that scrapes were used by mature bucks to locate does. New research indicates that this might not be the case.

One key element to a hot scrape is the presence of an overhanging limb. For a buck to use a scrape, there must be a limb hanging over the scrape. For at least ten years I (DS) have hunted near a scrape on some land in Ohio. That scrape is opened early and is continually hit by bucks. In fact I nailed a good buck near there several years ago with my bow. That scrape is located along an old grown-up road bed, now a barely visible trail. Three years ago a guy came through (illegally) on a tractor and plowed over the overhanging branch. My buddy, Denny Crabtree, went in and wired up a new overhanging limb. That scrape never missed a beat, and the bucks are still using it. Deer researcher, John Ozoga was right when he stated that the "overhead limb is the most important part of the scrape."

Remember, about half of the bucks that come to scrapes don't do a thing. They are passive. Other bucks exhibit various behaviors at the scrapes (as do some does). Two common behaviors are marking the overhanging limb and rub-urination. Bucks that come to a hot scrape will often (1) smell the ground, then (2) stretch high to the overhanging branch and (a) lick it, and/or (b) thrash their antlers and the base of their horns in it (probably exposing the forehead gland and the preorbital gland to the branch). Josh Braun, graduate student at Missouri State University, found that 57 percent of the interaction with the overhead limb involved rubbing the corner of the eye (preorbital gland), while 24 percent involved the forehead gland. Thus, it appears that *the preorbital gland is very important in deer communication at the scrape.*

Once that is done, he will probably paw the scrape and then bring the knee joints (the hocks) of his back legs together and urinate over them. In so doing he is urinating over the tarsal gland that is located on the inside of the knee joint. Often the buck will then lick the tarsal gland. This urinating behavior is called rub-urination and it is done by both sexes and can be seen all year round. But it is most prominently done by bucks at scrapes just prior to the peak of the rut.

Sequence of a buck visiting a scrape.

Buck smells the characteristic overhanging branch above the scrape.

The buck paws at the ground.

The buck urinates into the rejuvenated scrape.

Josh Braun found that the full marking sequence of marking the overhead limb, pawing the scrape, and rub-urinating in the scrape is done by bucks in less than 4 percent of their visits.

The why of rub-urination is all about odor. There are sebaceous glands under the tarsal hair producing lipids that cover the tarsal hair. These hairs then retain some of the components of urine and deer can then expose all these odors in response to encounters with other deer. It all sounds rather complicated, chemically, and it is. The key though is that rub-urination in bucks is tied to his testosterone levels and the doe's estrogen levels. In other words, it's all about breeding. You can observe deer rub-urinating most anywhere, but it usually occurs at a scrape. Charles Alsheimer, Christian friend, and the best deer photographer in the country, has observed that mature bucks do not seem to rub-urinate at scrapes in

October, but rather splay their legs as they urinate. Then come November, when the reproductive action really starts, the bucks will urinate using the rub-urination posture. Since the odors created by the combination of urine and sebaceous glands under the tarsal gland are very strong, his observations make sense. You would expect them to create these odors by rub-urinating more right before the peak of the rut.

Dr. Karl Miller also made an interesting observation in his breeding pens at the University of Georgia. He observed that subordinate bucks did not rub-urinate as frequently as dominant bucks did. When he removed the dominant buck, the younger bucks rub-urinated more frequently, but did not increase other activities at scrapes. When he put the big guy back, the little bucks stopped rub-urinating.

Table 1.

Behavior of 18 bucks, 36 does, and 9 fawns seen in scrapes.

Behavior Seen	Bucks	Does	Fawns
Smell the limb	10	24	6
Lick the limb	4	16	3
Rub eye on limb	2	0	0
Rub forehead on limb	1	0	0
Smell scrape on ground	13	22	6
Paw the ground	5	2	2
Urinate in the scrape	6	1	1
Auto-erotic behavior	2	0	0

Dr. Grant Woods kept details on 63 deer observed in scrapes; 36 does, 18 bucks, 9 fawns (Table 1). Ten of 18 bucks smelled the overhanging branch, and four licked it. Interestingly 24 of 36 does seen in scrapes smelled the overhanging branch and 16 of them licked it, but only the bucks rubbed their preorbital or forehead gland on the overhanging branch. Most bucks and more than half the does smelled the ground. The fact that only five bucks actually pawed the ground when visiting the scrape may have a lot to do with the age of the visiting bucks. Subordinate bucks probably paw less than dominant older bucks.

Woods also found that lots of does visited the scrapes. Because so many does smelled or licked the overhanging limb, he concluded that "does are actually depositing or detecting pheromone(s) on overhanging limbs." Note, they smell and lick the limb, but do not rub it with the preorbital or forehead gland.

I (RZ) also looked at behavior at scrapes. I took 96 deer photos on remote cameras placed at two scrapes (5 miles apart) from December to February in Texas. Seventy-seven of those photos showed bucks and 25 of those bucks actively interacted with the scrape (they stood over the scrape and pawed, rub-urinated, and/or rubbed their preorbital glands on an overhanging branch.) Fifty-two of the bucks in the photos were passive, showing no interest in the scrape.

The average age of the bucks (based on the appearance of 28 identifiable bucks in the photographs) was 5 years. Yes, a lot of mature bucks came to the scrapes. Of the bucks judged to be at least 4½ years, 16 of their visits (44 percent) were considered passive. Of the bucks judged to be 3½ years or younger, six of their visits (86 percent) were considered passive. OK, the sample size is small, but it appears that older bucks get more involved with the scrape than younger bucks. We should note that in this study area, there are a lot of older-age class bucks. However, as we shall see in a bit, in some other parts of the country, a lot of younger bucks come to scrapes.

Scrapes are universal property, thus visited by a number of different bucks including does and fawns throughout the breeding season.

Josh Braun monitored scrapes in Missouri with cameras and classified interactions as (a) no interaction, (b) interaction with marking, and (c) interaction without marking. He found that fawns were more likely to interact more, followed by bucks, then does. Does interacted about half as much as bucks. He also found that the younger the bucks the less likely they would interact with the scrape. For example, 40 percent of all yearling bucks marked the over hanging limb, while 50 percent of all 2½ year-old bucks, 52 percent of 3½ year olds, and 63 percent of all 4½ year-old bucks and older marked. Since we indicated above that rubbing the preorbital gland is done a lot at scrapes, then it's obvious that the preorbital scent is very important for older bucks. Why? Don't know, but it is.

Alexy, in a Georgia study we will discuss in detail later in this chapter, monitored six scrapes with video cameras 24 hours a day for two breeding seasons. Thus, she was able to determine behavior at the scrapes. She observed that when looking at the times when bucks interacted at the scrape (and ignoring the times when they were passive) they almost always marked or licked the overhead branch. Again, from the above research, it becomes apparent that they are licking odor from the preorbital gland. In less than half of those active visits did they paw or urinate in the scrape. And when this pawing or urinating did occur it was more likely to be seen in late October and early November. She also saw many does marking the overhanging limb. All of these observations led her to conclude that the overhead branches are especially important for chemical signals. The fact that does also marked the overhanging branch led her to suggest that does receive information about bucks at the scrape and by interacting with the limb they give scent information as well.

Full scrape sequences involve licking the overhanging limb, pawing and urinating in the scrape. These sequences were only seen 22 times in the two years of her daily observations. Twice as many of these were done by older bucks than yearlings.

Are there different types of scrapes?

Years ago two bowhunters, as good as any deer hunters that ever carried bows, wrote classic books on hunting big bucks. Gene Wensel, from Montana at that time, wrote "Bowhunting Rutting Whitetails". Roger Rothhaar, from Ohio at that time, wrote "In Pursuit of Trophy Whitetails". (Interestingly both now live and bowhunt in Iowa, which tells you something about big bucks in Iowa). These books contained a ton of observational information on scrapes and I still go back and reread them every two years or so, because their observations are excellent relative to learning about scrapes.

They talked about several kinds of scrapes, especially "primary" and "secondary" scrapes. These books were written by bowhunters almost thirty years ago. They weren't scientists, yet today we still talk about primary and secondary scrapes. Secondary scrapes can yield some good bucks because they are located along well used deer trails, and often lead into a good funnel. In other words, such scrapes are good indicators that a mature buck is in that area, and may be using the trail where the scrape was made. In fact, one can sometimes find a scrape line, with a series of scrapes along a trail that runs between bedding and feeding areas.

However, the scrapes that really mean something are the primary scrapes. Primary scrapes are like traditional rubs. They are made in the same spot year after year. Rothhaar noted that such scrapes were sometimes like the hub of a wheel. Instead of being made along a trail as most scrapes are, the trails come to the scrape. Because of this some outdoor writers use the term "hub" to define this type of scrape. Some hunters and outdoor writers call primary scrapes, "hot" scrapes, simply because lots of does come to them and lots of bucks can be seen in the vicinity, the two weeks prior to breeding. The Wensel and the Rothhaar books, now out of print I might add, go on to explain the importance of finding and hunting near such primary scrapes.

There is a third category of scrapes. As you walk along an old logging trail, or along the edge of a field, you can find scrapes under overhanging branches. You may also find them near fields where trails intersect. These look like hot spots, and it is tempting to hunt over such scrapes, but usually these scrapes are visited at night so hunting there is fruitless. These scrapes only tell you that a buck walked by and pawed the ground. Usually such "boundary" scrapes are made by younger bucks and mean very little.

There are some writers and hunters who do not put much faith in categorizing scrapes. They simply note that scrapes may be active or inactive and go from there. We don't agree and what follows is the latest science on scrapes. Read on and then draw your own conclusions on what scrapes mean and how you might use them to your advantage.

When during the fall do bucks scrape?

You won't find many scrapes in September, but when you do a mature buck probably made them. Check out the primary scrapes in your area, and watch for early activity. That will give you a clue as to whether that big buck you hunted last year made it through the winter, spring, and summer. Yearling bucks tend to open scrapes in mid to late October, but the big guys may hit them earlier, not often, but watch for early activity.

Research shows that the peak scraping time for the northern half of the country is the last week of October and the first week of November. For example, John Ozoga recorded the frequency of scraping in a 600-acre deer enclosure in northern Michigan. In the spring he located and tagged 26 scrapes scattered throughout his enclosure. They all had been pawed the previous fall. Starting October 7, he checked these scrapes every-other week until December 17. If the scrape was pawed, he put leaves on it except for a 10-inch circular area in the middle. All new scrapes found during his walks were also covered with leaves. Ozoga found that scraping jumped sharply the last week of October and peaked the first week of November. Eighty percent of all scraping occurred before the first female was bred in his enclosure (November 8).

In a second study, Ozoga walked a selected route within the enclosure. Twenty scrapes used the previous fall were marked and monitored from October 8 to November 12. Each week the ones that were pawed were recovered with leaves. Fifty-one new scrapes found while walking the route were also monitored. As you can see the peak scraping period in this enclosure was the first week of November, but the last week of October was also a busy one (Table 2).

Table 2.

The number of old scrapes reopened each week and the number of new scrapes opened each week in an enclosure in northern Michigan.

| Week | Old Scrapes | | New Scrapes | |
	Number	Number Pawed	Number	Number Pawed
Oct 8-15	20	2	7	7
Oct 16-22	20	6	20	15
Oct 23-29	20	8	30	12
Oct 30-Nov 5	20	10	48	23
Nov 6-12	20	9	51	7

Karen Alexy, a graduate student at the University of Georgia, conducted the most enlightening study ever done on scrapes. She used video cameras with infrared night lighting, placed at six scrapes in two northeastern Georgia counties. The areas studied had been under a quality deer management program (protect small bucks, shoot lots of does) for many years and the area had around 40 deer per square mile. Scrapes selected were ones that had been used in previous years. Four of the scrapes were along the edges of fields and two were in forests.

The results of this two-year study changed the thinking of many about scrapes. For example, she found that yearling buck visits to scrapes were highest from October 8-October 14. Wait a minute, yearling buck visits? Previously we believed that yearlings just didn't fool with hot scrapes. They may make some inconsequential scrapes, but they don't visit scrapes that are in the same spot year after year. Those are just for the big boys. Wrong.

Alexy learned that for bucks 2½-years old and older, the peak week was October 15-21, with October 8-14 in second and the first week of

Hunting over scrapes would be an effective way to see mature bucks,
except that most visits are made after dark.

November third in number of buck visits per day at scrapes. (Note the rut in this area is two-three weeks after mid-October). She also found rather heavy visitation rates the first two weeks of December. Most December visits were passive with little interaction at the scrape, but they did come to the scrapes.

The highest scrape visitation rates for does occurred in mid-October.

Where do bucks scrape?

The first scientific publication on where bucks scrape was in 1977. Those authors found scrapes where there was little understory vegetation, along game trails, old roads, or small openings. Most research since that time agrees that scrapes are usually placed in conspicuous locations, with little understory and on level ground. Since scrapes serve in deer communication, it makes sense that they need to be easily found by other deer. John Ozoga goes one step further and notes that scrapes are found where there is lots of deer activity.

What time of day do deer visit scrapes?

Grant Woods on a wildlife management area in Missouri did one of the earliest studies that looked at the time bucks came to scrapes. He found that most visits were at night. However, of the daytime visits to scrapes, the top period was from 8:45 AM to 10:15 AM, and the next most active was 3:45-5:15 PM. A third weaker period was from 11:45 AM-1:15 PM. Woods felt that in the morning bucks were more likely to scent check the scrape from downwind, rather than actually come to the scrape. During the late afternoon peak, bucks often came to the scrape rather than stop downwind. They also noted more behavior, such as rub-urination, pawing, etc. in the late afternoon visits. We know of no other studies that recorded behavior at scrapes during different times of the day. We can only speculate why there was more activity in the late afternoon. Does continuously hazed by bucks during the night become reticent to leave protective cover during he warmer daylight temperatures, affording deer a respite from intense pursuit. In other words, when the does bed down, bucks do the same (possibly a method of conserving energy). Hence, daytime visits to scrapes are diminished.

The Alexy study previously mentioned also found that most buck visits were at night; in fact she found that 85 percent of buck visits and 75 percent of doe visits to scrapes were at night. Dr. James Kroll, in a mock scrape study in Texas, found that half of bucks 1½ and 2½-years old and one-fourth of older bucks were photographed at the mock scrapes in the daylight. It appears that the older the buck, the less likely they'll visit scrapes during daylight. But wait.

I (RZ) took 48 deer photos with a remote camera at one scrape from Dec. 9, 1998, to Jan. 17, 1999, and found that *25 bucks visited that one scrape*. Fourteen of those bucks were judged to be 4½-years old or older and half of their visits were during the day. I also photographed deer at two scrapes about five miles apart from Dec. 6, 1999, to Feb. 12, 2000 and got 96 deer photos of which 77 showed bucks. Forty-five (58 percent) of those visits were at night. One very old buck was photographed at one scrape five times: four times at night and once during daylight.

Who comes to the scrapes?

For years we believed that a scrape generally represented the breeding season activity of one, probably older and bigger, buck. At the very least, we believed that hot scrapes, the good ones, were only pawed and visited by mature bucks. The advent of the remote camera has shown that these "facts" aren't reality.

Karen Alexy's camera study changed our thinking on this. She utilized motion-activated video cameras and red-lensed floodlights to record deer visits to scrapes over 24-hour periods. Results showed that not only do mature bucks visit these hot scrapes, but yearlings do as well. In fact, yearlings did 42 percent of the scraping. Bucks 2½+ years marked at scrapes during 51 percent of visits. She also noted that females made more visits to scrapes than males, but the males interacted with scrapes more often.

Apparently *dominant bucks do not control hot scrapes*. Just as was seen in Texas, Alexy saw as many as 13 different bucks and as few as three using one scrape in one year. We also formerly believed that once a buck came

196 • Whitetail ADVANTAGE

to a scrape, he would return and remark the scrape. That might be true for some bucks, but Alexy found that *only half of the bucks revisited a scrape*. She did have several bucks that revisited the same scrape six or seven times. But for the most part, only a few bucks visited more than one of her monitored scrapes, even though there were two that were only 300 yards apart. In fact she recorded only one individual that came to both scrapes.

Other studies have had similar results. Dr. Kroll's mock scrape study found no individual bucks revisiting a scrape during his research (which ran the last two weeks of October).

As mentioned above in the "What time of day do deer visit scrapes" section, I (RZ) had 48 deer photos taken at one scrape from Dec. 9 1998 to Jan 17 1999. The photos recorded 41 different deer at this single scrape of which 25 were bucks and ten of those were yearlings, one was middle-aged and 14 were mature, meaning they were at least 4½-years-old. Data from two other scrapes located five miles apart showed that 10 of 28 identifiable bucks visited the scrapes more than once. Two bucks visited the same scrape more than twice. One buck visited the same scrape three times, and another visited the same scrape five times. So even though there were more mature bucks on this site than on the Georgia sites mentioned above, only 10 bucks visited scrapes more than twice. As previously mentioned, maybe bucks can wind check the scrapes without actually having to come to them.

I (RZ) found a much higher number of older bucks coming to scrapes on my Texas study areas than Alexy did on her Georgia study areas. The fact is that there are many mature bucks on our Texas study area, probably many more than found on the Georgia sites. The older age class structure may explain why some of my bucks visited scrapes several times, while this did not occur on the Georgia sites. One conclusion can be gotten from both the Georgia and the Texas study. A scrape does not "belong" to any one buck, but rather is communal property that is visited by several individuals for a variety of reasons. It also seems obvious that seeing a buck at a particular scrape is no guarantee that it will return. And if it does, there's a good chance —around 50% or more —that the visit will be at night. However, one other important conclusion from these studies, hot scrapes attract lots of different bucks and does.

Grant Wood, in his master's thesis, stated, "At all of the monitored scrapes, younger and or smaller bucks (assumed to be subordinate) appeared to be as active in marking behavior as were the dominant bucks. On three occasions, bucks of different size or age classes were observed together in a scrape performing one or more of the scrape-associated behaviors."

Alexy had one other very interesting finding in her camera study of scrapes. Some bucks 3½ years and older did not visit the scrapes at all. She reached this conclusion because almost all of the 3 ½+ year-old-bucks harvested on her study areas were not videoed at the scrapes. In fact several older bucks were harvested quite close to monitored scrapes leading her to believe that these older bucks wind checked the scrapes without visiting them.

Then again maybe a few big bucks didn't visit scrapes at any time. My (DS) friend, Gene Wensel, told me several years ago that he was hunting a buck that for whatever reason, did not participate in the rut. In other words, Gene didn't find any rubs or scrapes made by this buck, never saw him make rubs or scrapes, and never saw him chasing does. Other whitetail specialists have also indicated a similar belief — there are older whitetail bucks that don't seem to be interested in does. And in chapter 10 we discussed what bucks do the mating, and studies have shown that some older bucks just don't mate does. Hmmm.

Do Mock Scrapes Work?

Yep, they do. In the late 80's and early 90's there was a lot written about mock scrapes, but in recent years we don't hear as much, probably because guys tried them and they didn't work. Well, we are here to tell you that mock scrapes may not be a magic elixir, but they can attract bucks. In those

Rattling at artificially established scrapes enhanced by the application of doe in estrus urine is an extremely effective technique to deceive a mature buck.

early mock scrape days, what was written came from hunters. There was no science on mock scrapes. There still isn't much science out there, but what has been done shows that mock scrapes do attract deer.

Bob McGuire, a bowhunter from Tennessee, started the whole mock scrape idea. Bob went to great lengths to keep his human odor away from the scrapes he made. Bob Fratzke was another bowhunter, from Minnesota, who wrote a lot about making scrapes. Both hunters talked about the licking overhanging branch above their mock scrapes. Both noted the advantages of hunting near mock scrapes as opposed to hunting near the real ones.

When you build a mock scrape you can take advantage of wind, better cover, and you can create a licking overhead branch that works. The other advantage is that you can start them early. Some hunters, including Bob Fratzke, start them in late spring. Bob simply makes an overhanging branch, and then scrapes the area under it. As he notes, when the first buck comes to that branch and scrape that scrape goes from being a mock scrape to a real one. He believes that if the mock scrape isn't used, you built it in the wrong place. He also believes that *you should make 3-4 mock scrapes close together as this attracts bucks better than just one scrape.*

To make the overhanging limb, you can simply bend and wire a small sapling so that the top of it is 4-5 feet over the scrape. Or you can actually wire or nail a small sapling to a nearby tree so that the tip is over the scrape. Wear rubber gloves and never touch the end of the sapling where the deer will lick and smell. Deer researcher John Ozoga erected 40 artificial overhanging limbs in his large research pen and 24 of them became scrapes within 5 weeks. He then did another test where he created overhanging limbs, opened up the leaves, and also put doe in heat urine in some. Neither removing leaves nor adding deer urine increased the rate at which bucks scraped beneath his artificial limbs.

There have been few scientific studies of mock scrapes. Dr. James Kroll and Ben Koerth conducted the most interesting mock study ever done.

From October 11 to December 5, they put infrared-triggered cameras on mock scrapes with various scents placed in them. In 1998 they created four replications of mock scrapes; one set had nothing in them, one set had rutting buck urine, one set had doe-in-heat urine, and one set human urine. The results were interesting especially for those of you who believe that human urine scares deer.

Bucks visited scrapes with buck urine and human urine the most. Estrus doe urine and scrapes with no scent came in a close second. The researchers could not distinguish a statistical difference in visits to these scrapes, and they saw no difference in the age of bucks visiting these scrapes.

The next fall they made mock scrapes with buck urine, hot doe urine, no scent at all, and some with "new car scent" spray. Again the results were a bit unexpected. Bucks came to all four treatments. The fact that bucks came to new car scent spray, and to mock scrapes with no scent was attributed to curiosity. Dr. Kroll found that almost as many does and fawns came to the scrapes as bucks. Does came more to the doe estrus urine than the other treatments, while bucks seemed to favor the estrus urine and the buck urine. It appears then that a scrape can bring bucks to it based on visual signals (they came to a scrape with nothing in it), *and* scent signals. In addition, they obviously come out of curiosity (e.g. new car scent spray).

Several other researchers have studied the use of mock scrapes in deer pens of various sizes. Again, they found that bucks often came to the scrapes. Some had no scent placed in them, others used hot doe urine. These studies tell us that we should at the very least, scrape out a mock scrape every time we get in a tree stand. Put it on a location where you will not have bucks wind you when they come in, and where you want to shoot when they see and/or smell the scrape.

Before ending this chapter, let me add something on preorbital glands and overhanging limbs. All the above research shows that the preorbital gland scent is important at scrapes. Some friends of mine from Pennsylvania have been using preorbital gland lure at primary scrapes and mock scrapes for the past few years. (Google "preorbital gland lure" to find where to buy this. It is expensive because it is collected from the preorbital gland of harvested bucks). They start applying the lure to overhanging limbs in August, and do it weekly through October. Their results have been nothing short of fantastic and I am now a believer. They've harvested some super bucks in Pennsylvania on or near such scrapes. My Ohio lease friends put it on two primary scrapes that are hot every year. Using preorbital gland lure made those scrapes hotter than ever, and we saw and photographed more bucks there this year than ever before.

There you have the latest scientific data on scrapes. Maybe that is more dirt on scrapes than you bargained for, but our advice is to store this information away and use it when you have a hunting situation where you need some answers.

Hunter: *Apparently there are different kinds of scrapes. Some are built along trails, while others have trails that go to the scrape (in other words, the scrape is opened and so many deer come to it that trails develop). Which ones should I be hunting?*

Dave/Bob: *The primary scrapes mean more than others because they are used year after year. However, if the wind isn't right, then you might not be able to hunt a scrape, no matter what kind it is. Scrape and rub lines can be great places to hunt, especially if they lead into, or come from, a funnel. Sit the funnel. Again, the wind has to be right, but if you find scrape and rub lines near a funnel, you have a gold mine.*

Hunter: *If bucks scrape at night, then isn't it a waste of time to hunt near scrapes?*

Dave/Bob: *Not really. Remember, studies show that in Georgia 15 percent of the visits are in day light. But, the Texas data are even more revealing. Two different studies there showed that half the bucks come during the day. And in my (RZ) camera data, many bucks over 4½-years-old came during the day. From this it appears that older bucks may visit a fair amount in the day. Remember also that often you can't sit near a primary scrape because of the wind. So, you may sit away from the hot scrape, near a very active trail. This isn't a bad idea, because even if big bucks don't come to scrapes in the day time, during the rut, they are active, especially at dawn and dusk. The hot scrape may tell you that a big buck works that area. Being on a nearby trail could be the answer when he walks by, even if he isn't going to the scrape.*

Hunter: *What if the overhanging limb gets broken?*

Dave/Bob: *Replace it. Either pull down a nearby limb so that it is positioned 3-4 feet directly above the scrape, then wire it in place. Or cut off a nearby limb and wire it above the scrape. The same goes for mock scrapes. The overhanging limb is critical to attracting bucks to scrapes.*

Hunter: *You stated in the previous chapter that bucks like to rub aromatic trees. What do you think of the idea of attaching a limb from an aromatic species such as cedar and making it the overhanging limb?*

Dave/Bob: *I think that is a super idea, and I know of at least one hunter that uses this approach with great success.*

Hunter: *I had no idea that does spent so much time at scrapes. And they lick the overhanging limb a lot too. What is that all about?*

Dave/Bob: *Scrapes are all about communication. Does talk to bucks via odor at scrapes, and apparently bucks talk to does and to other bucks via odor. They will lick and rub the overhanging branches every month of the year, but come November they paw and urinate as well.*

Hunter: *It seems as though mock scrapes have merit. You presented data that showed that some bucks come to mock scrapes even if there is no scent placed there. So, what do I do to get bucks coming to mock scrapes?*

Dave/Bob: *Several things. First, as the one study showed, build three mock scrapes close together as that seems to attract more bucks than single scrapes. Second, every time you get into your tree stand you should at least scrape away leaves under an overhanging limb within bow or gun range of your treestand. Putting hot doe urine or buck urine in them is probably better, but if you are running late and need to get off the ground in a hurry, just quickly kick away the leaves. It just might stop that buck where you can get a shot.*

Although much concern is focused on Chronic Wasting Disease, blue tongue (Epizootic Hemorrhagic Disease) is devastating to deer, particularly northern deer.

CHAPTER 13

Your Future with Chronic Wasting Disease

C hronic Wasting Disease was first found in mule deer in a research penned facility in Colorado in 1967 and then in 1981 it was found in the wild in that same state. Since 1967, the spread has been slow, but steady and if you examine Table 1, you can see the evolving history of this disease as it moves about the country. From that chronology, it is obvious that things started slowly, but in the past six years Chronic Wasting Disease has established a major foothold in wild deer and elk in many parts of the country.

In fact, today it is found in the wild in deer, elk, and moose (just one animal) in Colorado, Wyoming, South Dakota, Nebraska, Kansas, Wisconsin, New Mexico, Utah, Illinois, New York, West Virginia, Saskatchewan and Alberta (see Table 2). It has also been found on a number of farmed cervid facilities in Alberta, Colorado, Kansas, Minnesota, Montana, Nebraska, New York, Oklahoma, Saskatchewan, South Dakota and Wisconsin (see Table 3).

Table 1.

The Chronological History and Spread of CWD.

1967 found in captive research facility in Colorado Foothills Wildlife Research Center in Ft. Collins. Later called wasting disease because deer appeared to be "wasting away".

1977 Beth Williams finds brain is spongy in appearance and determines deer disease to be a transmissible spongiform encephalopathy (TSE). (She formerly was the veterinarian for the state of Wyoming, but was killed in a tragic automobile accident in 2006).

1980 found in captive mule deer and elk in a wildlife research facility in southeast Wyoming.

1981 first recognized in free ranging elk in northeast Colorado in Rocky Mountain National Park. Later, in free-ranging elk in Wyoming, then in free-ranging mule deer and white-tailed deer in Colorado and Wyoming.

1986 found in elk in wild in Southeastern Wyoming. By 2001, 10 % of deer in that part of Wyoming had it.

1989 CWD-positive elk shipped from South Dakota to Saskatchewan game farm. That animal died in 1990.

1990 Colorado starts surveillance of hunter-killed animals.

1996 Elk on Saskatchewan game farm found positive for CWD

1996 new variant of Creutzfield Jacob Disease (a transmissible spongiform encephalopathic disease (vCJD), found in British people. From exposure to TSE by eating infected cattle products. Now recognized to have caused death in 130 people in England.

continued

1997 South Dakota first state to find CWD in commercial elk herd. Two more herds found positive within one year. Surveillance of game ranched elk begins in many states and provinces.

1998 found in commercial elk herd in Oklahoma.

1998 game farm in Nebraska found with CWD.

1998 second farm in Saskatchewan with CWD

1999 animal in Montana game farm tests positive.

1999 Wisconsin begins to test because of game farm problems elsewhere.

2000 first wild mule deer with CWD found in Saskatchewan.

2000 found in wild mule deer in Western Nebraska. Also found in Nebraska elk game ranch.

2001 USDA issues a declaration of emergency regarding CWD Begins plan to eradicate disease on game farms and in the wild.

2001 29 Saskatchewan game farms under quarantine as CWD animals or those from ranches with CWD were moved around. Eventually 8,000 elk were killed, 100 positive.

2001 game farm in Nebraska has 43% of its deer test positive.

2001 whitetail deer in wild found CWD positive in Nebraska, near a CWD + captive elk herd.

2001 one white-tailed deer in wild found CWD positive in southwestern South Dakota.

2001 quarantine placed on 11 game farms in Colorado.

2001 CWD found on Kansas game farm that had earlier received an elk from Colorado farm that was from a farm that subsequently became quarantined.

2001 found in two wild mule deer in Saskatchewan.

continued

208 • Whitetail ADVANTAGE

2002 seven year, $8.4 million dollar research project started at Colorado State University focusing on how the disease spreads from deer to deer. Also working on vaccine.

2002 CWD found in mule deer in Colorado west of the Continental Divide.

2002 three white-tailed deer test positive in Dane County, Wisconsin.

2002 mule deer within Denver city limits positive for CWD.

2002 CWD confirmed in Alberta farmed elk.

2002 mule deer at White Sands Missile Range tests positive.

2002 found in farmed elk in Aitkin City, Minnesota.

2002 Oregon bans import of elk or deer. Meat needs to be deboned. Several other states doing this. New York is one of those states to ban imports.

2002 female deer in Illinois tests positive.

2002 permanent import ban on live elk/deer in Oregon. Done in many states.

2002 found in another wild mule deer in Saskatchewan.

2002 elk from Wind River National Park in South Dakota tests positive.

2003 six deer from Nebraska panhandle test positive.

2003 three more Illinois deer test positive.

2003 more deer in South Dakota test positive.

2003 three more deer in New Mexico test positive. Herd there is 150.

2003 deer found positive in northeastern Utah.

2003 research in Colorado shows that more bucks get CWD than does.

continued

2003 test results from hunting season coming in. Nebraska had 12 deer test positive from Sioux County. South Dakota tested 1950 deer and elk and now has a total of 9 positive deer and one elk. Virginia tested 1100 with no positives. Michigan tested 3315 wild deer and elk and 55 game farm deer and none were positive. Washington tested 1500 deer with no positives.

2004 found in new area in Nebraska, 250 miles east of original contaminated area.

2005 five deer from two game farms in New York test positive. Two in wild also positive.

2005 research strongly suggests there is a barrier that may well prevent spread of infected prions from deer to humans.

2005 a buck in the wild from West Virginia's eastern panhandle tests positive.

2005 five more deer in the wild from West Virginia's eastern panhandle test positive.

2005 Alberta starts culling wild deer along Saskatchewan border in efforts to keep CWD out of wild herd. Fifty-seven deer have tested positive right across border in Saskatchewan.

2005 some deer from that effort tested positive in Alberta.

2005 found in wild deer in three new distinct areas in Wyoming.

2006 four more deer in the wild test positive in West Virginia's eastern panhandle.

2006 CWD prions found in leg muscles of deer.

2006 first deer to test positive on a game farm in Minnesota.

2006 first wild moose tests positive in Colorado.

2007 five more deer with CWD in West Virginia's eastern

Table 2.

The States/Provinces and Year CWD Was Found in the Wild.

Colorado	1981
Wyoming	1997
Saskatchewan	2000
Nebraska	2000
South Dakota	2001
Wisconsin	2002
New Mexico	2002
Illinois	2002
Utah	2003
Kansas	2005
New York	2005
West Virginia	2005
Alberta	2005

Table 3.

Captive Cervid Facilities Where CWD Has Been Found.

States Where CWD Found on Game Farms as of 2005	Number of Farms where CWD Animals Found * **
Colorado	14
Kansas	1
Minnesota	2
Montana	1
Nebraska	4
New York	2
Oklahoma	1
South Dakota	7
Wisconsin	7
Saskatchewan	Many different farms

*12,000 animals tested in 2003, 15,000 tested in 2004.

** 31 elk herds, 8 whitetail herds

Chronic Wasting Disease is not your average deer disease. It is different and scary because it is a disease of the brain and because it is similar to "Mad Cow" disease. It is that similarity that concerns hunters who fear they might contract the disease by eating contaminated wild deer just as some people contracted "Mad Cow" disease by eating beef. More on eating venison later.

Prior to 2002, few hunters had heard of Chronic Wasting Disease (CWD). Once it crossed the Mississippi River into Wisconsin, and once 8,000 elk had to be killed on Saskatchewan game ranches, CWD took on a new meaning. No longer was it someone else's problem. Now it was east of the Mississippi River and it had the potential to be the new kid in everyone's neighborhood.

Background Information About CWD.

Before getting to specific questions about the disease, let's look at a little history and other negative aspects of this new disease. CWD is a brain spongiform disease. The name comes from the appearance of the brain (spongy, full of holes) from animals that are infected. There are a number of brain spongiform diseases, most affecting animals. Scabies in sheep is one that has been around for almost 200 years, while "Mad Cow" disease has been around for only a short time. But the fact that around 130 humans died in Great Britain from eating beef that was infected from being fed brain tissue from animals that had spongiform disease raised the concerns about Chronic Wasting Disease. If humans could get one spongiform disease from eating animals, could they also get Chronic Wasting Disease from eating infected deer or elk? The answer to date is no, but it's still one huge and scary question.

The other frightening factor about CWD is the effect it potentially could have on deer and elk herds in the wild. You see, once an animal is infected, it dies. It may take several years to show up, but the animal will die. Since biologists from Colorado (where CWD was first found in captivity and in the wild) and Wyoming now believe that without management CWD could wipe out all deer and elk in an area, and since they also believe that density of animals increases the prevalence of CWD, the scare has even more ramifications.

One of the problems in following CWD is that it can remain latent in animals for long periods of time, perhaps as long as five years, before it becomes expressed and the animals die. If so, will we see it spread into more states? Almost assuredly. Even with strict controls on game ranching and heavy culling in the wild in hot zone areas, CWD will continue to spread. Could it eventually spread to all whitetail habitat? This is a distinct possibility.

The major concern of Chronic Wasting Disease is the fact that young deer can have it, but do not demonstrate its effect until they are much older.

How Did CWD Originate?

The cause and transmission of CWD remains a bit of a mystery. Contaminated tissues are the brain, spinal cord, lymph notes, the tonsils of deer (but interestingly not the tonsils of elk), blood, saliva, and muscle tissue. Through extensive and innovative research, it was discovered that infected brain proteins called prions caused the disease. In ways we do not understand some of these prions occasionally go "bad" and then in some way the disease spreads to other animals. But, what caused these prions to go bad? Some feel it happened spontaneously. Some believe it jumped the species barrier. For example one thought is that Scabies in sheep jumped to deer and/or elk. (They were studying Scabies in sheep in the research penned facility where deer first showed signs of CWD in 1967). Others believe that the cause is a bacteria that affects the brain proteins and is transmitted via an insect (hay mites).

Researchers at two Universities suggested that the disease was stimulated by environmental factors. Those environmental causes were postulated to be low copper or high manganese in the diet. The causes for low copper and high manganese were several, from over browsing by too many deer or elk in an area, to over fertilization of fields, to high use of insecticides, to placement of road salt to melt winter snow and ice.

Needless to say, studying these theories is very challenging. One needs to be an expert in neuropathology, nutrition, soil chemistry, animal pathology, bacteriology, etc., to follow these theories. That's hard enough for a scientist working in one of these disciplines; it is impossible for hunters or others just trying to understand the disease.

How Is CWD Spread?

Research shows that if you put healthy deer in a pen with CWD deer, the healthy deer get CWD. If you put healthy deer in a pen where CWD animals formerly lived, they also get CWD. And if you put healthy deer into a pen with contaminated deer carcasses that have been aged for many months, some get CWD.

There is other research. For example, scientists from the Wyoming Fish and Game Department took brain material from CWD elk and orally inoculated low, medium, and high doses into healthy elk. All died or were killed when they exhibited terminal CWD symptoms. Those that died did so around 650 days after exposure to CWD with the high dose group dying slightly faster than the medium and low dose groups. Interestingly 8 of the 10 elk in a control group held in adjacent pens also got CWD, indicating indirect transmission of the disease.

Formerly it was thought that the disease was only spread by direct animal-to-animal contact, but a research study in the online Journal of Emerging Infectious Diseases indicates that CWD can spread through environmental contamination, without live animals being present. In this study CWD infected deer were placed in a pen, then removed for awhile. When healthy deer were then placed in the pen, some came down with CWD. Though we'll never find densities of infected deer at these levels in the wild, this still shows that CWD can spread via something left in those pens (feces, nasal drippings, saliva, etc.).

We've always known that CWD prions were in the brain, but we now know that prion agents spread from the brain to the tongue via sensory and motor fibers. Researchers looked at the tongue because it has many nerve endings associated with the mucosa. They found the prion agent in elk tongue, and hypothesized that their presence there could mean that prions are shed via saliva. If that is true, and it sure appears to be so, baiting, or any activity that brings high numbers of deer together to feed, can accelerate the spread of CWD in the wild.

For the last several years there has been concern that *hunters who place deer urine in scrapes might be exacerbating the problem*. Not so. New research shows that CWD is spread via saliva. In that study healthy deer

216 • Whitetail ADVANTAGE

were exposed to urine from deer with CWD, and none got the disease. However, when other deer were exposed to saliva from CWD-positive deer, all got the disease within 12 months. All fawns given blood from CWD deer got the disease within 12 months, but of importance to hunters using doe urine, no deer exposed to urine and feces from CWD deer got the disease. We already knew that the prions went to the tongue and now we know that saliva is involved.

Three years ago I had a game rancher tell me that no wild deer have ever been found dead with CWD. The insinuation was that CWD may infect wild animals, but not kill them. This is not true. At a CWD Symposium in 2005, researchers reported CWD in a wild dead deer found in a farm field in Saskatchewan, a male spike elk in South Dakota, a mule deer in New Mexico, and a mule deer in a farm field in Utah. We find prevalence rates in the wild as high as 15% (in parts of Colorado) and CWD deer have died in the wild in every state where it has been detected.

CWD Has Been Around Awhile and Populations Are Fine, So Will It Ever Hurt Our Deer Populations?

While it is true that it has been out there for quite a few years, the latest computer models show that once your state or province gets the disease, if left unchecked, you could get local extinctions of deer. When CWD rears it's ugly head, deer in that area must be harvested in larger numbers. There are no other options.

What Percentage of Deer Have CWD?

In most places in the wild where you have the disease, probably only 1-3 percent of deer have it. However, there are hot spots in Colorado where as many as 50 percent of deer have the disease. Again, the answer here is to lower deer and elk numbers.

In the hot zone in Wisconsin the adult prevalence for CWD in 2002 (first year after CWD was found in Wisconsin) was 6.7 percent. In 2003 the prevalence was 5.3 percent.

If a State Samples and Tests 300 Deer, and All Are Negative, Does This Mean There is No CWD There?

Based on those sample sizes, your state may have it and they may not. Here is why we say that. Right after CWD entered Wisconsin; biologists there determined that if only one percent of the deer had CWD, you'd need to sample 500 deer *per county* to have a 95 percent chance of finding it. Population density and size of the county play a role, but in general these data show that you need very large samples (thousands) to determine whether CWD is present in a state. In 2002, many states tested less than 1,000 deer. A good start, but to be sure there is no CWD in a state, you probably need to test several thousand deer.

Are Some Deer More Susceptible to CWD?

The answer is "yes." Researchers from the University of Wisconsin, Utah State University, and the Colorado Division of Wildlife reported that the prevalence of CWD increases with age of deer. Males are also more likely to get the disease than females (buck prevalence rate was 7.4 percent, female rate was 5.4 percent). There is also a difference with age. The older the deer, the higher the probability of infection. And, the increase in the preponderance of males getting the disease as they age (e.g. 13 percent in $3\frac{1}{2}$-year-old males) was twice the rate as found in females (7 percent).

The authors point out that the increase in the prevalence of CWD, as the deer age is typical of a disease where the risk of infection increases with the time of exposure to infected animals. Obviously, the older a deer gets, the number of deer they have interacted with increases.

They also found some fawns with CWD and postulated that there is a lot of contact with the mother for several months after birth and that is the likely source of the disease.

How Can You Tell If A Deer Has CWD?

Some deer are found in the wild that look and act sick. In the late stages of the disease deer may lose bodily functions and show abnormal behavior such as staggering or standing with poor posture. They may carry their head and ears lowered. They may drink large amounts of water and drool and salivate. They will look thin and just appear to be wasting away (actually it is this appearance that caused the woman who first found the disease to call it "wasting disease"). However, most deer with CWD show no symptoms and they may not show signs of infection for years.

One problem with this disease is that we don't know the incubation time. Some deer show signs of the disease and die when young, while others do not show signs of the disease until later in life. Almost certainly some old deer that have the disease die without showing any symptoms. The fact that the disease can incubate for years makes a full understanding of CWD difficult.

The characteristics of Chronic Wasting Disease are quite similar to other diseases and also not unlike the appearance of this battle-worn buck.

What Will Kill the Prions Once on the Ground?

Apparently not much of anything. The bad prions that cause this disease in deer and elk are just about indestructible. They can be buried for up to three years in the soil (maybe longer, but so far the research has only gone on for three years), and still be able to spread the disease. The prions have been placed in autoclaves and heated to very high temperatures, and they still survived. There apparently are some chemicals that one can use to kill the prions, but these would obviously not be practical in the wild.

Then How Do We Get Rid of Contaminated Carcasses?

States where CWD is common, such as Wisconsin, have been wrestling with this for several years. The best method would be to put the carcasses in some type of metal container that would remain sealed forever. However, that just isn't practical from a financial perspective. Wisconsin has been dealing with hundreds of contaminated carcasses. They've reached the conclusion, as have other states and provinces, that land filling is the only way to deal with dead deer with CWD. Incineration is done in some cases, but for the most part, CWD-positive deer and elk are placed in land fills. The only way deer could come into contact with bad prions via a land fill would be water runoff, and the way most landfills are designed, that would be highly unlikely.

Will CWD Be Eliminated Via Hunting?

If we've learned anything over the past six years it is that hunting will not eliminate CWD. When CWD was first found in Wisconsin a "hot" zone was created where deer numbers would be lowered to such a level that CWD would not spread. After several years, with the continuing spread of CWD, it is obvious that this approach has not been totally successful.

220 • Whitetail ADVANTAGE

When Chronic Wasting Disease first hit Wisconsin in 2002, the DNR liberalized hunting, especially in an eradication zone, in efforts to eliminate the disease. Early on they talked about eradication. That word alone caused concern. The proposals to eradicate deer in a 411-square-mile hot zone and to stop all baiting alienated many hunters. Though the kill in the hot zone was good, it was far less than needed. In fact deer populations were still 30-35 deer per square mile after the 2003 season. (A more recent study shows that in 2003 each hunter in the hot zone shot an average of 1.71 deer. Seems like they just needed more hunters there).

There are several reasons why *hunting will not eliminate CWD*. First, completely eliminating a wild deer population in a fairly large area is not possible. As more are shot, the remaining deer become extremely wary. Second, hunters will help, but as deer numbers and hunter success drops, interest wanes. Hiring sharpshooters is expensive, and the revenues lost from the eruptions of CWD makes the economic situation even worse for state DNRs. There are localized instances where deer numbers may be lowered to a level where CWD will disappear, but in general it can be said that hunting will not eliminate CWD.

How might the deer harvest be increased? Recent studies done at the University of Wisconsin at Stevens Point show that hunters would not utilize introducing a financial incentive program with money given to hunters who take deer. That study also showed that a only a minority of hunters supported the original reduction goal of 5 deer per square mile, and most believed you could not eliminate CWD by hunting. That indeed has proven to be true.

Interestingly the 54 percent of hunters who didn't support the DNR reduction goal were just as likely to hunt a lot and shoot more than two deer, as were the hunters who supported the DNR. Studies show that the number of deer a hunter is willing to harvest for their own use is related to deer seen and shot opportunities, rather than time spent hunting, attitudes toward management, or concern about the disease. The Earn-A-Buck program (where a doe must be harvested before a buck can be taken) motivated many hunters to harvest a doe, however, this program was not popular with hunters and reduced the enjoyment many hunters got from hunting. Bottom line is that hunters will shoot more deer if the opportunity is there (I. e., if they see more deer), but only if they are able to use the meat.

Will Lowering Deer Numbers Slow the Spread of CWD?

Yes. Since CWD is spread from one deer to another, either directly or indirectly, the fewer the deer, the less chance you have of an infected deer encountering an uninfected deer. There is no question that the strategy of hammering deer in zones where CWD appears is sound and necessary. Shooting deer in hot zones is not a cure, but it definitely slows the spread. In fact, in very localized situations, lowering deer numbers may completely eliminate the disease. New York may be an example. In 2005 the disease was detected in five captive and two wild deer in Oneida County. Since that time harvest has been increased and 1,800 deer from the CWD Containment Area were tested and found negative.

What Will Happen If We Do Nothing?

The CWD experts all agree that doing nothing is not an option. Most experts feel that going about our deer hunting business as if there wasn't a disease in the deer herd, could be a potential disaster. No one knows for sure, because no state has tested and found CWD, then just walked away and said, we have it, no problem. States that find CWD in their wild herds shoot deer. The agency shoots deer, hunters shoot deer. They do so because there is a chance that CWD will do serious damage to the entire deer herd and no one wants to take that chance.

When a state finds CWD, they implement the plan that almost all states already have in place. This involves more surveillance, more testing, removing deer, and monitoring game ranches. (For a summary of the latest testing, state-by-state, go to Table 4).

Is Baiting An Issue?

While we are talking about how CWD is spread, let me interject how baiting may play a role in all this. The postulation is that baiting brings deer together in high numbers, hence aiding the transmission of the disease. Studies show that bait sites (and supplemental feeding sites as well) bring animals together and this may increase the chance for direct contact or indirect contact via saliva, urine or feces. This then may increase the transmission of CWD (actually urine is not a factor. more on that in a minute).

Consider this study. Researchers took CWD-free deer and exposed them to saliva, blood, or urine and feces from CWD positive deer. Deer exposed to saliva from deer with CWD all got the disease within 12 months. This in part explains the concern game agencies have about baiting and the spread of this disease.

Although baiting deer represents a viable management technique, when it comes to enhancing harvest success, concentrating deer makes them more susceptible to disease.

We described the new study that showed that CWD prions are found in saliva, and not the urine. Since deer lick each other, graze in the same area where saliva may be deposited on grass, and eat at the same bait sites, the chance for spreading CWD via baiting is obvious.

Baiting has become a major political football in Wisconsin. Hunters feel that baiting increases success and they fight to keep it legal. But studies show that baiting doesn't improve the success rates for gun hunters very much, but it does for archers. This then means that stopping baiting (not just in Wisconsin, but in many other states), even if it is shown to be a part of the CWD problem, will be difficult. The DNR in Wisconsin wants to stop baiting, but the hunters and the feed stores want to keep baiting. Yes, baiting in Wisconsin is big business. One study showed that 450,000 bushels of bait were used in northern Wisconsin during the 2001 deer season. That works out to be a huge eight bushels per northern deer hunter that baited.

Right next door, in Michigan, baiting is also a hot potato. The fact that baiting and feeding wildlife in Michigan is a $50 million dollar business makes elimination all the harder.

Some related baiting news. The National Shooting Sports Foundation recently reported a 31.8 percent prevalence of CWD from 69 deer sampled in a Colorado urban community where feeding is common. This has led some to suggest that baiting has caused this high prevalence, but there is no way to prove that this is the case.

Manitoba has banned all baiting for deer, elk, and moose. In fact, you cannot hunt within 0.8 km of bait. Even further, if you leave crops for deer bait, you cannot hunt there and law enforcement can either force the planter to remove the crops or fence them in. Manitoba has taken the baiting issue one step further. You cannot use urine, feces, or scent glands from deer to aid your hunting. You can't even own such products in Manitoba.

A rule of thumb on baiting is that politicians support baiting, while game agencies oppose it. Thus, when the Mississippi legislature introduced a bill to legalize baiting, people got nervous. However, common sense prevailed as the legislature decided to ditch that bill and pass one that puts such a decision in the hands of the Commission on Wildlife, Fisheries and Parks. It is refreshing to see the legislators in Mississippi deciding to let the experts make a wildlife decision. The bill allows the Commission to study the impacts of deer baiting and then make a determination. The Governor agreed and signed the bill into law in April 2007. Meanwhile, in 2007, Nova Scotia made it illegal to use deer urine even though it has been shown that urine does not spread the prions.

Are Game Farm Escapes and Releases a Problem?

There is no question that a few CWD positive animals are escaping from game farms. A survey published in Wisconsin in 2003 showed that over a 5-year period, 671 whitetails had escaped from one-third of the 550 deer facilities over the lifetime of the farms operation. Only half were ever recaptured. What is troubling is the fact that some of the escaped deer came from farms with CWD, and at least one was known to have the disease. As another example, two elk shot on public land in Utah were tagged and traced as escapees from a nearby game ranch.

When the markets for game-farmed deer and elk began to decline, and when feed costs rose, a few unscrupulous game ranchers released stock into the wild. It is possible that some of these animals were infected with CWD. Two such releases took place in Wisconsin, and at least three such releases have taken place in Alberta. In one case involving 28 elk released northeast of Edmonton, all were subsequently shot and fortunately none tested positive for CWD. The good news is that we don't hear stories of dumped animals any more.

There is no question that game ranching is a part of the CWD problem (see Table 2). Nowhere has this been more evident than in Saskatchewan where CWD was first found in farmed elk in 1996. We know that the first contaminated animals were shipped to a game ranch in Saskatchewan from a farm in South Dakota. If you follow the dots, it can be seen that from that one Saskatchewan farm, approximately 40 other farms were contaminated via shipped animals. Thousands of game farmed deer and elk were destroyed and more than 22,000 wild-killed deer were tested

If Captive Deer Do Not Show Symptoms of CWD For Three Years, Then Is It Safe to Move Them to Game Farms in Other States?

This is not true. Though game ranchers want the ability to sell deer and move them across state lines, the way CWD works puts those deer and elk ranchers in a bind. What isn't known is the incubation period for CWD. Unless you can definitely prove that a deer does not have CWD, any movement across state lines could spread the disease.

Will A Fence Around A Game Farm Prevent The Spread of CWD?

There are several problems here. First, as already noted, a few deer and elk escape from game farms. Second, if wild deer come in contact with penned sick deer, saliva might be exchanged leading to spread of the disease. A fence will not necessarily prevent this from happening though it does make it unlikely. Third, the prions that leave the body in saliva remain in the soil for years. It is possible that heavy rains could wash these prions through a fence. Double fencing would reduce that risk, but when this is proposed, game ranchers resist because of the expense. That expense is very real.

Is CWD Spread From the Wild to Game Ranches or is it the Reverse?

Since we know that saliva is one source of the disease, a wild deer with CWD could lick a deer inside a fence and thus spread the disease. However, since the prevalence of CWD on some game farms has been found to be high, most infections probably started on deer farms. Circumstantial evidence supports this. In at least one instance state DNR officials equally sampled wild animals in concentric circles around a game farm that had the disease. The further one sampled from the ranch, the fewer the occurrence of CWD. In other words, wild animals close to the ranch had a high prevalence of CWD, and it decreased the further one got from the ranch. The obvious source of the CWD in that area was the ranch.

Is There a Barrier That Will Prevent Moose From Getting CWD From Deer or Elk?

Lets first look at what we know. The prevalence in wild deer is much higher than the prevalence in wild elk. We also know that prion protein levels in the lymph nodes in the throat area are much higher in deer than in elk. We know very little about moose and CWD, but during the 2006 hunting season one hunter-killed moose from Colorado was found to be positive for CWD. Having said that, CWD levels in moose will probably be quite low and stay that way simply because moose have little interaction with deer or elk. And we don't find large herds of moose, as is the case with deer and elk. Thus, the chance for saliva transfer is greatly reduced for moose.

Can Humans That Eat Meat From CWD Positive Deer or Elk Get CWD?

Of course, this is the big question relative to CWD. However, research shows that there is a barrier between elk and humans and deer and humans relative to prion transmission. Will that barrier always be there? There is no way to know. The scare is based on the fact that "Mad Cow" disease is a prion caused sickness in cattle that jumped to humans. Though relatively few humans have died from "Mad Cow" disease, the potential is always there and it did happen.

However, based on several studies it now appears *very unlikely that humans can contract CWD*. We've been hearing this all along, but now there are data to show that humans probably cannot get CWD.

Oingzhong Kong and other researchers from Case Western Reserve University used inoculated mice with various types of prion proteins and concluded that "there is a robust species barrier for transmission of elk or sheep-adapted CWD prions to humans." Further research is being continued, but this work is optimistic to say the least.

Gultekin Tamguney and others at the University of California's Institute for Neurodegenerative Diseases established lines of mice "that express a prion protein that is common to mule deer, white-tailed deer, and elk". They inoculated the brains of mice with these prion proteins and found that the mice were equally susceptible, regardless of what cervid was involved. They also infected mice that expressed human prion proteins with CWD prions from deer and elk and found high resistance. This is great news.

As a further indication that the meat is safe, note that CWD has been in wild deer and elk in Colorado since at least 1981 (the date it was first found in the wild). In 2004, over 800 of 25,000 tested deer and elk harvested by hunters in Colorado had CWD. Another 50,000 deer and elk were harvested that were not checked. Most were probably eaten by hunters. That means that as many as 2,400 CWD positive animals may have been eaten by hunters in Colorado that year. Obviously many were eaten the previous year, and the year before that, etc., etc. My estimate is that as many as 20,000 CWD-positive deer and elk have been consumed by hunters in Colorado since 1981, and no one has gotten ill from doing so. No guarantees, but it looks good.

Even so, Patrick Bosque from the Denver Health Medical Center noted that we need to continually monitor those who have eaten CWD-positive deer or elk to make totally sure that such transmission will not occur over time. In fact, all of the researchers who reported on this issue indicated that we need to do more work. Thus, although the above data show it is very unlikely that humans will contract CWD, more time is needed before we can rule that out. Having said that, understand that hunters and their family members have eaten thousands of CWD positive deer and elk for many years with no ill effects to date. The disease has been in Colorado and Wyoming for many years, and hunters have eaten elk and deer from diseased areas for many years, with no known problem. Will that always be the case? Again there is no way to know, but this situation could hold the key to the future of hunting. If only a few hunters would die from eating CWD positive deer or elk, hunter participation would decrease. At a time when game agency budgets are stretched to the limit, and at a time when hunter numbers are decreasing, any further decrease could be a major problem. Do we think this will ever happen? No.

Can Game Agencies Afford To Handle Any CWD Problem That Might Arise?

Not really. Not without eliminating or seriously curtailing other wildlife programs. Hunters talk a lot about game agency budgets, especially when the agency requests a hunting license increase. If you listen to some hunters, the game agency has more money than it can use. The truth is that most game agencies are having budget problems, and if CWD does enter a state, other wildlife programs will have to be cut or eliminated. Since 2002, Wisconsin has spent $26 million in the battle with CWD. Expenses involve testing deer (for a sample of just how much testing is being done, see Table 4), disposing of contaminated carcasses, culling deer, educating the hunting public, etc. They even had to construct a facility to process the thousands of deer heads each year.

My own home state of West Virginia has CWD in one county. Administrators indicate that if CWD pops up in other regions of the state, the finances to fight the spread are just not available. What this all means is that hunters need to support DNR-based tactics to prevent CWD from spreading. No question, CWD has changed the deer management landscape, but we've lived with this disease for awhile, and with prudent management, we can continue to do so.

Table 4.

These are the latest testing results for CWD, as of May 2007.

Alberta
During 2006-2007 hunting season 2000 deer tested, of which four mule deer were positive. Total positives for the province now numbers 29.

Delaware
Of 1,900 deer tested since 2003, no positives

Florida
2300 deer tested, no positives.

Illinois
6,733 samples taken in 2006, with 41 new positives. Have found 167 positives since 2002

Iowa
4,579 tested in 2005, with no positives.

continued

Kansas
Collected 10,737 samples since 1996 with one positive from an elk ranch in November 2001 and one wild doe killed by a hunter in December 2005.

Maine
Over 900 samples tested in 2006, all negative.

Maryland
About 3,700 deer tested since 2002, all negative.

Massachusetts
577 tested in 2005, no positives.

Missouri
As of 2005, no positives.

Montana
Since 1998, have sampled 10,600 deer, elk, and moose with no positives.

Nebraska
133 wild deer positive from samples from 33,000.

New Hampshire
1,890 deer tested since 2002, no positives.

New Mexico
15 positive deer since 2002.

continued

New York

Since 2002, 18,700 samples tested, including 1,800 from the containment area from April 2006 through March 2007. There were five positives in 2005, but no other new cases.

North Carolina

1,800 deer checked since 1999, with no positives.

North Dakota

Tested 8,500 deer and 147 elk since 2002 with no positives.

Ohio

1,097 samples taken in 2006, no positives.

Oklahoma

2,834 tested, with no positives as of 2004. Has since been found.

Pennsylvania

4,260 samples taken in 2006, no positives.

Saskatchewan

68 positives in wild deer as of July 2005. Many positives on many game farms.

South Dakota

72 positives (52 deer, 20 elk) found since 1997. 17,188 wild deer and elk tested.

Tennessee

No positives found. No private ownership of deer allowed.

continued

Utah

Nearly 12,000 deer and elk have been tested since 2002 with 33 mule deer testing positive of which 24 came from the LaSal Mountains, and five from the Vernal area. In 2006 they tested 1,934 mule deer of which seven were positive. Five hundred elk samples were negative

Vermont

276 deer tested in 2005, no positives.

Virginia

800 deer tested in 2006, no positives.

Washington

All samples negative.

West Virginia

Found eight more positive deer, bringing total to 19 and all in Hampshire County in eastern panhandle.

Wisconsin

129,019 deer tested since 2002, 834 positive.

Wyoming

4,653 deer, elk, and moose were tested in 2006, with 116 positives including 88 mule deer, 13 whitetails, and 15 elk. 36 moose tested, none positive.

---

* Note: the fact that all states are not listed does not mean that they have not been checking dead deer for CWD. Some of the above information was taken from **www.cwd-info.org**. Some states have not listed updated information on that site, nor could I find it elsewhere, so they are not included.

What Needs to Happen Where CWD Is Found?

When CWD is found in most states or provinces, the state wildlife agency goes in and attempts to remove a rather large number of deer around the site where the contaminated animal was found. This lowers the chance for spread, and also gives the state animals to test for CWD.

In states where larger numbers of CWD animals have been found, successful efforts have been made to lower deer numbers. In many areas we have more deer than the habitat can sustain, and lowering deer numbers, though it upsets some hunters, will slow the spread of CWD.

Excessive deer populations are not only detrimental to habitat, they are more susceptible to diseases like CWD.

Knowing All The Above, What Should I, As A Hunter, Do?

There are several things that hunters can do to attack CWD. First, wear rubber gloves and bone out the meat. These prions are found in the brain, spinal cord, lymph nodes, blood, muscle and the tongue. Although there is no evidence that venison isn't safe, these precautions should be practiced until we learn more about CWD. Bone out all deer meat and you will not only have better tasting venison, but it should be safe to eat.

What can you do to prevent CWD from coming to your property?

Until we know more about how CWD is spread, this is a difficult question. However, there are several things that you might do. If you bait or feed wildlife, do so in small one-two gallon amounts and move the feeders or bait stations around so body liquids do not build up in the area. Using smaller amounts will also decrease the numbers of deer that may come to the stations at one time. Our thoughts are that three small bait stations in one area are better than one big bait station.

As quality deer management programs increase, more bucks will succumb to natural causes and old age. This is particularly evident on trophy management operations.

One method of reducing the probability of disease is the reduction of deer populations by harvesting does. As a result, a more natural balanced sex ratio will develop, but some bucks, like this one, will still perish as the result of increased competition and fighting.

It is a plain and simple fact (even though some hunters don't see it that way), that we have too many deer in most areas. Lowering deer numbers not only makes deer habitat stronger ecologically, but it also yields an overall healthier deer herd. Thus, the most important thing you can do to protect your herds from Chronic Wasting Disease, is lower deer numbers.

If you lease your farm to hunters, require every member to utilize all the doe permits they can get in your state. Some lease groups go so far as to oppose all doe hunting. This is medieval thinking in most areas. If there are twenty hunters in the lease, and each legally can buy permits to take two does, then require the lease club to harvest forty adult does on your property. If your property is large enough to host twenty hunters, it probably can sustain a doe harvest of forty a year. Eliminate shooting all fawns, because half of them are bucks and bucks is what the lease members want to shoot. If some members do not want to hunt does, require the club to bring in friends or family members for a doe hunt. Bottom line, harvest more adult does. If your hunt leasers do not understand the value of harvesting many more does, then get hunters that will understand. Taking more does will not only increase the health of the herd, it will lower your tree damage, increase the quality of bucks, and lower the chance for the spread of disease.

Support political advances asking for more money for CWD research. The more we know about CWD, the better the future of hunting. Fourth, support the temporary ban on moving deer and elk from state to state. Once we learn more about how CWD is spread, we may not need this safeguard, but until then this precaution is needed.

Finally, we need to relax and just go hunt. There can be little doubt that in 2002, fears about CWD caused some hunters to stay out of the woods. The antis love CWD. In response, you and your friends need to get out there and hunt.

Hunter: *It appears that CWD is a "new" disease. Are there other diseases that have popped up in the past 30-40 years?*

Dave/Bob: *As a matter of fact there are. In the early 1970's we heard whispers about the possibility of bovine tuberculosis in deer. In the 1990's it surfaced. This disease is transmitted from one deer to the next by direct contact of saliva, either nose to nose, or on infected feed.*

In 1975 the first case of Lyme Disease was found in Connecticut. Though this disease does not affect the deer directly (they carry the infected ticks), the prevalence of this disease has increased rapidly since that time.

Hunter: *Since we've had several new deer diseases pop up that seem to arise and spread when deer densities get high, will there be new diseases down the road?*

Dave/Bob: *We believe there will be more, new, deer diseases. Today we really manipulate deer a great deal. We breed them; we feed them; we buy and sell them; we collect sperm; we maintain very high numbers in the wild (this might be the scariest factor of all). There is a lot of artificial "management" going on out there and we believe that this will lead to more diseases in the future.*

Hunter: *Is there a place where I can check on the latest state regulations for my own state?*

Dave/Bob: *Yes. Go to www.cwd-info.org and then click on your state or province from the map. This then gives you the regulations for your state including laws on transporting carcasses, baiting, and CWD testing. If you just want the regulations, click on "regulations" on the home page.*

Seeing that first buck regardless of its size is a memory that endures forever.

CHAPTER 14

Trophy Hunting;
Our Perspective

This chapter is a bit different in that both Bob and I have written two separate pieces on trophy hunting. But our philosophy on trophy hunting is the same. We both feel that trophy hunting has gotten a bad rap in the media and is very much misunderstood, not only by non hunters, but also by many hunters. Maybe they see an image of the rich, illegal hunter who wants to kill the biggest animal at all costs. Though that may be what trophy hunting is to a few, it is not what trophy hunting is to most and it never has been. This chapter discusses what we believe trophy hunting really is. We've written it because the mental image most people have of trophy hunting differs from our real-life experience hunting quality animals. Here are our thoughts on the values of trophy hunting.

Why I'm Proud to be a Trophy Hunter
by Bob Zaiglin

As the forests' distorted figures began taking shape at dawn, I found myself situated with my back against a fallen yellow poplar. It was the first day of the 1970 Pennsylvania deer hunting season, and the entire affair was invigorating.

At 18 years of age, sleep had been out of the question the night before, but a rush of adrenaline now eclipsed all weariness. Although I knew deer could detect movement with radar-like abilities, I constantly rotated my head in search of a buck. I scanned the forest floor, and imagined bucks at various positions between the mature hardwoods. Finally, I caught a glimpse of a deer browsing on the understory.

It was headed in my direction.

In minutes, the deer appeared within 50 yards of my position. I immediately saw antlers, but never counted the points because I knew the buck was legal. Inundated by intense excitement, I remained cemented in position until the buck moved behind a large oak tree that obscured its vision. I slowly eased over, placed my gun on a decaying log and waited for what I hoped wasn't an apparition.

Once the buck stepped from behind the huge oak, I positioned the crosshairs on its shoulder—an image I had admired in magazines like *Outdoor Life* and *Field & Stream* since childhood—and gently squeezed the trigger. As my first buck, a 5-pointer, tumbled to the ground, my excitement escalated to an uncontrollable level. I had accomplished a dream, the memory of which is permanently etched in my mind.

My first buck wouldn't have scored high on the Boone and Crockett scale, but it remains as much as trophy to me as some record-book bucks I've taken.

Hunting, and more specifically, deer hunting, has always been an inherent passion of mine. Even when I was too young for a license, I watched in admiration as hunters clad in ubiquitous red plaid pursued rabbits near my Pennsylvania home.

After the first few days of deer season, I would check out the back yards of men I knew hunted whitetails. December in Pennsylvania is cold, and in the late 1960s, hunters traditionally hung deer in their back yards for several days before butchering.

Shooting a buck of Boone & Crockett proportions is a dream shared by all sportsmen and experienced by a lucky few.

Since those days, I've enjoyed an exciting career as a wildlife biologist. I earned a bachelor's degree in wildlife science from West Virginia University and a master's degree in range and wildlife management from Texas A&I University. My education, followed by a lot of hard work, opened doors I never knew existed. At age 27, I was managing large tracts of prime deer country in central and South Texas.

As a wildlife manager in Texas, it wasn't long before hunting mature deer affected me. My definition of a trophy changed as my skills improved and my opportunities increased. Over time, I evolved into a discretionary hunter.

As a youngster, I was elated to see a buck, let alone shoot one. As I learned more about deer behavior, I became better at locating them. I learned deer sign, used the wind to my favor, positioned myself where visibility was good, and more importantly, hunted where deer lived.

Although I killed several antlered deer in Pennsylvania and West Virginia, I always dreamed of seeing one of those super rare bucks sporting a rack of B&C proportions. At age 25, I entered a new stage in my hunting development. I defined a trophy buck as one that was at least 4 ½ years old with a rack obviously larger than anything I had previously shot. Under these criteria, my chance of taking a trophy in Pennsylvania was slim, particularly when 80 percent or more of the state's buck harvest was comprised of bucks younger than 2 ½ years.

When I moved to Texas, it was easier to elevate my standards because older bucks existed there. Before long I learned more about the mature white-tailed buck.

I had no desire to shoot my limit of two bucks. Instead, I wanted to kill a single, highly desirable buck each year if I could find one. Once I enjoyed the taste of success, I continued to raise my standards until my goals became almost impossible. Because of this, I found myself shooting fewer bucks. A true trophy hunter often comes home with great memories, but no buck.

Most hunters will take smaller bucks during their early years. But as they mature, some hunters will have a desire to raise their standards, searching for larger racked bucks.

Trophy hunters demonstrate much interest in deer management. At this level, sportsmen are concerned with sex ratios, age-class structure, and more importantly, the animal's nutrition. As a result, trophy hunters are dedicated to managing the land and the animals they hunt. Even though I enjoy hunting trophy deer, I always take my limit of does to maintain a naturally balanced sex ratio, and because my family enjoys the venison.

I also find myself continually experimenting with basic habitat to enhance the nutritional quality of a deer's diet. Being a trophy hunter is a year-round commitment that includes removing excess does during the

Many deer hunters, particularly trophy hunters, are managers knowledgeable of deer and their requirements, thus they are more than willing to harvest surplus does, collect harvest data, and establish food plots to benefit the animal.

The number one objective of the trophy deer hunter is to pursue deer where at least the possibility of seeing a buck larger than he has ever taken exists.

hunting season, searching for shed antlers in spring, and creating food plots in late summer and early fall. Trophy hunters put a lot of time and effort into their sport.

Obviously, the number one ingredient for shooting a trophy buck is to hunt where the bucks exist. It's not only the kill that drives the trophy hunter; it's also the satisfaction of knowing a trophy buck is actually out there.

Anyone can get lucky and shoot a trophy-class buck, but hunting for a free-range buck with exceptional antler qualities requires skill. For example, one of the ranches I hunt is 100,000 acres, which makes hunting a challenge. Also, when you consider a trophy buck makes up less than 5 percent of the buck herd, it's easy to see how difficult it is to kill one.

Put another way, there is about one adult deer per 25 acres on the ranch, and the doe-to-buck ratio is 1½ to 1. About 4,000 deer inhabit the area, with 2,400 does and 1,600 bucks. It sounds like a surplus of bucks until you consider that only 30 percent, or 480, are mature and only 5 percent, or 24, are actual trophies. Finding one of these 24 elusive bucks is the challenge trophy hunters cherish. Hunting on the ranch is particularly challenging because baiting is not permitted.

Success is the crossroads where skill (complemented by luck) and opportunity meet and the harder a sportsman works at honing his skills, generally the luckier he gets.

There is a big difference between a trophy hunter and a trophy collector. Hunting where the kill is guaranteed is not characteristic of the dedicated trophy hunter, but of the collector. Where and how the sport is pursued is important to the trophy hunter. The trophy hunter considers small, confined high-fenced herds unsportsmanlike and unacceptable. Fair chase is paramount to the trophy hunter's ethics.

Knowledge of deer and their environment is crucial, but luck plays the greatest role. I have always said I would rather be lucky than skilled. However, the trophy hunter must be prepared for anything. Success is the crossroads where skill and luck meet. The hunter might be lucky enough to see that outstanding animal, but his skills must be adequate to finish with finesse.

Whether a trophy hunter uses a bow or firearm, he must be a confident and competent marksman. Thus, practice is a principal component to success. A trophy hunter practices year-round with his weapon simply to fine-tune his shooting skills. It's a mortal sin among trophy hunters to take a questionable shot.

The trophy hunter strictly adheres to the old adage, practice makes perfect.

Possibly the most prominent characteristic of a trophy hunter is perseverance; that is, the ability to hunt long and hard for even a slim chance at success. The true trophy hunter also feels remorse after killing a buck because he respects what the buck conquered to reach the older age class. However, that remorse is only ephemeral. The hunter knows he has taken one of nature's rarest jewels - a trophy buck.

The truth is, bucks in trophy management programs have the opportunity to live longer. As previously mentioned, 80 percent or more of the bucks killed in many states are younger than 2 years old. In trophy hunting, a buck is allowed to age so its antler characteristics fully develop.

There is no negative impact on a herd when only trophy deer are shot. In fact, by allowing bucks to age, they breed more and ensure their genetic traits are perpetuated.

Trophy hunters compete with no one but themselves. They are proud of their accomplishments yet do not elevate themselves above those that lack the opportunities they have been blessed to enjoy.

Competition is not part of the trophy hunter's agenda because trophy hunters compete with no one but themselves. They are usually aggressive, but their hunt is a private affair. Success is considered a personal achievement.

Today, the public generally accepts deer hunting as a means of managing deer populations, but trophy hunting isn't. Some can't justify selecting the best animals only for their antlers.

There is no biological factor that makes a huge-racked buck the most superior animal in a given herd. In fact, a deer with exceptionally large antlers is an aberration, and there is no way to determine whether it carries any superior survival qualities over its cohorts. A trophy-sized rack is the exception, not the rule. The rarity of the animal is what drives the trophy hunter.

Trophy hunting is a privilege that must be nurtured. It's not for everyone, although it's a rare hunter whose heart does not beat at the sight of a huge buck.

I have taken some tremendous bucks in my life, but I still regard my first as one of my best. Even though it did not have a trophy rack, it was a trophy hunting experience. A hunt should never be measured by the size of the rack, but rather the quality of the experience.

—*Deer and Deer Hunting* magazine, 2002

My Perspective on Trophy Hunting;
Dr. Dave Samuel

Hunting has always given me a multitude of benefits. As Dr. Randall Eaton expressed, "I don't hunt to control game herds. Nor do I hunt to support wildlife conservation. If I did, I'd buy all the licenses, permits, tags, and stamps; then stay home and watch hunting videos. I hunt because I love to hunt." (In *"Tell It Like It Is,"* Bowman's Journal 1 (1), Autumn 1999). Yes, I hunt for the benefits, and there are many.

 Dr. Donna Minnis noted that, "describing hunting by labeling it as 'sport hunting,' 'meat hunting,' or 'trophy hunting,' depicts hunting as providing only one purpose" (e.g., for recreation, food, or trophy, respectively) (In *"Communicating A Pro-hunting Message: Pitfalls To Avoid,"* Proceedings Annual Conference of Southeastern Association of Fish and Wildlife Agencies, 1997). When we reduce hunting to just one dimension (e.g. "trophy hunting"), we do it a disservice. Hunting, even when you are after one truly outstanding animal, has many purposes that go far beyond what we call "trophy" hunting.

Hunting for quality animals is a part of my bowhunts for deer. I'll take the first legal deer I can to make sure there will be meat in the freezer over the winter. Then I will become selective and attempt to harvest a larger deer. In so doing, I will pass up many shots, observe lots of deer behavior, and spend many hours in the woods.

Some non hunters and hunters as well seem to think that trophy hunting is not ethical. However, equating illegal activities to the legitimate trophy hunter is like equating drunk drivers to all motorists who drive cars in a legal and safe manner. The real trophy hunter is actually one of the most ethical of all hunters, and understands nature and the outdoors more than most.

For some reason, many folks seem to think that trophy hunting is something that started with the modern gun hunter. Not so. In fact, the truth is that we humans evolved as trophy hunters. In 1978, Randall Eaton wrote a classic paper on "The Evolution of Trophy Hunting" in the very first issue of a journal called Carnivore. It is a classic article on this subject. His hypothesis was that man evolved not only as a hunting animal, but also evolved as a trophy hunting animal. The argument is compelling, and may help explain why modern hunters are so prone to put animals on their wall, antlers on the garage, bear claws around their neck, mounted animals in their office, etc.

His argument is relatively simple. Eaton believed that the highest social status went to primitive hunters who were the most fit and who killed the most and biggest animals while citing much scientific, anthropological literature to support his theory. He showed that male hunters benefited when competing for females if they advertised their hunting prowess.

For example, male members of the King Bushman could only marry after they killed a large herbivore. Another study showed that a female Bushman female could not marry outside her culture, but cited one exception when a male who was not a Bushman was allowed to marry a Bushman because he was an exceptional hunter. In short, good hunters had an advantage when seeking a mate and perpetuating their race.

Most early primitive peoples advertised their hunting success by displaying trophies. Most primitive peoples still do today. Eaton noted that the Akoa pygmies wore elephant hair bracelets. Bushman cut strips of hair from antelope they killed and made bracelets for their wives. Others could tell the species of the animal taken by the color of the hair on the bracelets.

More difficult trophies were then recognized as being taken by Bushman who saw the bracelets on the wives. There are other examples of how primitive hunters gained status and wives via hunting and killing trophies.

Mbuti pygmies killed large antelopes and gave them to the parents of the bride-to-be before the parents allowed a marriage. Alaskan Eskimos had to kill a series of animals, culminating with the polar bear prior to a completion of the marriage eligibility. Eskimos killed grizzly bears even though they were not used for food. Trophy hunting? Probably. Males became chiefs of the Sciriono peoples of the Amazon Basin based on their hunting abilities.

One could argue that chiefs and leaders of primitive peoples became such because their fathers were the leaders. In other words, they inherited their leadership. Eaton contented that good hunters became the leaders and chiefs.

One study showed that chiefs were selected by nonhereditary means in 13 of 18 hunting cultures but in non hunting cultures, chiefs succeeded each other because they were sons of chiefs in 93 of 160 such cultures. The conclusion? Good hunters became chiefs. Thus, there was selective advantage to being a good hunter. Eaton cited many examples where this was true.

Among Tikerarmiut Eskimos the most prominent males were those who hunt whales. The Nootka, northwest coastal Indians, hunted whales "as a test of valor." Various Indian societies of South America show the same thing - male status depends on hunting success. The Kayapo of the Amazon Basin hunted jaguars as trophies to prove their bravery. The Waiwai of the Amazon achieve status by hunting. Many Plains Indians killed grizzlies as a symbol of power.

Pastoral societies that raise livestock also must kill predators to protect their cattle. The males of those peoples (the Zulu, Suk, Turkana, Marakweet) wear leopard skins to advertise their trophy hunting skills. Examples could go on and on, but the conclusions are rather obvious. Since the best hunters got the most and best women, and had the highest social status among the males, such hunters probably had an evolutionary selective advantage.

They would breed more; they (and their families) would eat more protein and hence survive better. In other words, the best hunters, and the hunters who killed the biggest animals (i.e., the trophy hunters), would survive and would evolve.

The best hunters displayed bravery by killing large predators. This gave them status, but it also reduced competition in their hunting areas for prey. By reducing competition for food, there is again a selective advantage to being a good hunter.

But Eaton pointed out that killing large trophy predators might also be ritualistic, "done in such a way as to give individuals the opportunity to demonstrate warrior skills." Eaton also pointed out that paintings and sculptures of Paleolithic hunters emphasized the head, which suggests an emphasis on killing trophy animals.

Nootkan war chiefs used charred bone from wolves or mountain lions to paint their faces before raiding other Indians. Authors suggest that bone from these predators provided power. Even in war, the best hunters seemed to have the advantage.

Eaton also suggested that in some hunting cultures, art originated from hunting trophies. He also suggested, "picture writing could be traced directly to trophy art." His paper has an interesting discussion about the role of lion hunting in the evolution of the Pharaohs in Egypt and the importance of trophy hunting to the Greeks. Greek coins had hunting scenes on them.

He also noted that Plato advocated hunting as a part of the training of young men. Eaton even suggests that some dancing evolved from imitating "animals to enhance hunting success." He suggested that acting might have evolved from dance.

Eaton noted, "Eight different monarchies of Europe are symbolized by the lion (as are seven in Asia by the tiger)." He points out that we still utilize trophies as important symbols of society. Taverns known as the "Red Lion Inn," automobiles named after trophy animals like cougar, bobcat, mustang, and jaguar. We give "trophy cups" to people who win races, competitions, and Eaton suggested that this form of trophy may have originated in the late upper Paleolithic hunters of Europe, "who may have used trophy skulls as drinking cups."

Finally, Eaton pointed out that people today attack trophy hunting "as an expression of male ego" and he stated that this is biologically correct. "However, the moral judgment against trophyism is not necessarily valid," he said.

No question that reading Eaton's essay on how we evolved as trophy hunters presents some very compelling arguments and interesting ideas.

Perhaps the most basic question about trophy hunting is, is it ethical? Though humans probably evolved as trophy hunters, many in society today are opposed to trophy hunting. Even so, most hunters keep some form of trophies, whether it be antlers from last year's deer, or hides and furs from animals they have harvested. Some go one step further and make jewelry from their animals.

Some convert parts of the animals into art. Over the years I've had several western fringe leather coat made from deer hides. And, yes, I have a "trophy room." It is my den, where some of my best animals are located. In fact, I do all my writing in my den. It is a rather private place, a bit separate from the main part of my home.

Why do I keep such trophies? Is it because I want to possess the beauty of the animal? Is it because I want to remember the hunt? Is it something subtler whereby I subconsciously want to maintain my tie to my evolutionary past? Is it a way for me to let others know that I am a good hunter, a skilled hunter?

My guess is that keeping trophies is something that we do for all of these reasons. John Madson, in a paper given at the Montana Governors Symposium on North America's Hunting Heritage stated: "Ten thousand years ago the hunter might have stood by a fire and recounted the great

My trophy room is called the memory room as it allows me to recall all the sounds, smells and sights of each and every cherished event in my hunting lifetime.

deed to his clan brothers, while the old men nodded their approval and stripling boys back in the shadows listened in wonder. It hasn't changed much. The trophy hunter, the ethical killer of the great stag, or bear or ram, still commands attention by the fire as he recites his deeds. His peers still salute him, the old men still nod and remember, and boys still dream of tomorrow's hunts."

The 4th edition of the Pope and Young record book has two very important chapters on trophy hunting. *"The Truth About Trophy Hunting"* by Bill Krenz, and *"The Value of Trophy Hunting"* by Jim Dougherty, are both considered "must reads" for all serious hunters. These chapters point out that trophy hunting is misunderstood, and as I noted earlier, it is misunderstood by not only non hunters but by some hunters as well.

Anti hunters and others suggest that trophy hunting kills off the best animals and thus damages the herd. John Madson points out, "neither the mathematics of genetics nor the observed facts of breeding within wildlife populations add support to that contention."

You will hear this argument from anti hunters over and over in the future, but no scientific studies back up this claim. For the common species that we hunt there is no biological proof that shooting big animals affects the reproduction of the species in any way.

Jim Dougherty pointed out that trophy hunting is not the "fabricating (of) reputations" that a few hunters feel that they need to satisfy their ego. However, it is these guys that we read about; they give us all a bad name, they give trophy hunting a bad rap that it does not deserve.

Bill Krenz noted that trophy hunting is not a science but a philosophy. Trophy hunting has always been a philosophy. It was a philosophy for primitive peoples, and it still is today.

As Krenz pointed out, there is a big difference between a science and a philosophy. Anti trophy hunters think the science of killing is the same as the philosophy of trophy hunting. Not so.

Krenz noted that with science you have an "external reward" to prove your accomplishment. With a philosophy the reward is something internal, and it's hard to measure. The philosophy of trophy hunting doesn't involve ego as much as it involves honor, self respect, achieving something, and responding to challenge.

The key to trophy hunting is not the science, and it is not in killing trophies. It is the philosophy, the value to each trophy hunter, and the way it was done. The key to trophy hunting isn't the killing, it is the hunting, and the hunting is the philosophy.

It must be totally ethical, totally legal, and totally in keeping with good biology and good wildlife management. As Krenz and Dougherty point out, the most important aspect of trophy hunting is not the kill, but rather how we hunted.

The pursuit and who it is shared with, not the kill, is critical to the trophy hunter. In other words, the experience is not a measure of tine length, but rather the length of the hunt.

I'm reminded of a story told to me by brothers Gene and Barry Wensel about a huge buck they had hunted for at least a year. While bowhunting, one of them came upon that buck in the river and ice on the shore prevented the deer from getting out of the water. Eventually he did get out, but he could have been easily shot with a bow while in the water, while getting out, or once he was on land.

It was not done. No trophy is worth doing something unethical. To the true trophy hunter, ethical hunting behavior is paramount.

It is the hunter who decides what is a trophy. For my old friend, Keith Dana of Rock Springs, Wyoming, a trophy antelope is one that has abnormally shaped horns. Me, I want to hunt an antelope that has normal-shaped horns, but Keith will spend all year chasing a buck that has horns that point in directions that antelope horns normally do not. That is a trophy to him.

Some of us will only take big animals with long bows. Others won't use treestands. Others won't wear camo. A big doe might be a trophy to some. Some hunters hunt a certain animal all year long, even though it doesn't meet the Pope and Young Club or Boone and Crockett minimums for record book status.

A trophy has different meanings to different people. A few years ago my dear friend Ginger Fausel took her first animal with a bow, and it was a beautiful strawberry blond bear in Saskatchewan. It was not a big bear, but was it a trophy? Absolutely. The bear was a trophy in Ginger's eyes, and was taken in fair chase, by a bowhunter who is ethical in every sense of the word.

Do people cheat in this system? Eaton, in his article on *"The Evolution of Trophy Hunting"* suggested that primitive man probably cheated on occasion. A hunter would find a dead trophy, and take the horns to be displayed as his kill. Thus, he gained high status in his clan. We have cheaters today. The cheaters of today are the takers. The trophy hunters are the givers. They fight for hunting, and for the animals. They don't need to harvest animals all the time as they search for that one, sometimes big, trophy.

Real trophy hunters are not the problem with hunting today. They are ethical and have an ethical philosophy about hunting. As Bill Krenz pointed out, the philosophy of trophy hunting "aspires to make hunting more perfect." If all hunters aspired to that philosophy, than hunting would be healthier.

"The trophy-hunter is the caveman reborn."

—Aldo Leopold

Hunting is continually being challenged and is no longer a right but a privilege.

CHAPTER 15

The Future
of Hunting

I f you look at things from a short-term perspective, the future of hunting doesn't look all that bad. But when you go back 30 years, and look at the bigger picture, the future is fairly bleak. No, we won't lose it all, but the signs are fairly clear that we will continue to lose hunting, piece by piece, and bit by bit. Consider that in relatively recent years we've lost bait hunting for black bears in Washington, Oregon, Colorado and Ontario. We've lost hound hunting for mountain lions in Washington and Oregon. We've lost hunting of some species in Botswana, Zambia, and other African countries. We've lost hundreds of thousands of acres of wildlife habitat to housing developments, golf courses, malls, highways, etc. And we've lost access to thousands of acres of leased land and country farms owned by urbanites who want to protect their weekend retreats. True, there have been a few gains for hunting, such as a short, limited bear season in Western Maryland, but overall, the future does not look good.

Four Recent Negatives For the Future of Hunting

Example # 1. In 2006, in what might be the first instance in North America, Outfitter Leonard Ellis sold the license controlling the hunting rights to his 7,722 square-mile area to a group opposed to recreational hunting in that area. The Raincoast Conservation Society paid $1.35 million for the hunting rights in the coastal area in central British Columbia known as the Great Bear Rainforest. This move ends all guided hunting in that area. The purchase was made in cooperation with First Nations native groups living in the area.

At the heart of the issue is a desire to stop all bear and wolf hunting and replace lost revenues via eco-tourism. The area supports many wolves, grizzlies, black bear, and the Kermode white variation of the black bear. First Nation natives feel they can benefit more from eco-tourism and believe that is not compatible with sport hunting. According to an article in the Vancouver Sun newspaper, Ellis hunted this area since 1981, but now believes that certain regions of British Columbia should be open only to eco-tourism and others to hunting. Government regulations state that some hunting must be conducted, but this will be limited to resident hunting of hoofed animals on a reduced hunt-for-food basis. That same article stated that residents take 40 percent of all animals harvested in this area, but First Nation representatives are working to eliminate that as well.

This buy out does not bode well for the future of hunting in British Columbia. It demonstrates that there is big money available from non hunters to purchase hunting territories. Even though a Raincoast spokesman stated they only wanted to stop the hunting of bears and wolves, eliminating guides and outfitters from that region also means no nonresident hunting of mountain goats, moose, mountain lion, and deer. We know that in places like Kenya, where sport hunting was stopped in favor of wildlife viewing in 1978, revenues have not done as well as when there was hunting. Although it probably won't happen, because dollars from eco-tourism have not been all that good, there has been considerable efforts to get sport hunting legalized again in Kenya in recent years. Just as in Kenya, the chance of eco-tourism dollars replacing hunting dollars in this part of British Columbia is rather remote. Nonetheless, this huge area is now closed to most hunting. If non hunters can buy hunting rights in this area, they can do it in others. The money is there.

Example # 2. In November 2004, the Humane Society of the United States and the Fund For Animals announced a merger that will allow them to have a combined budget of $96 million to use on various issues. Of concern is the announcement that one of their major campaigns will be to stop bowhunting because bows are inaccurate and wounding occurs. The fact that these two groups want to abolish bowhunting isn't new. Joining together to do it doesn't change anything except to put huge money and more attorneys into the process.

The issues the animal rights groups have used to try to stop bowhunting remain the same. It isn't safe to use in suburban environments (yet no one has ever been injured in such bowhunts). Deer will run around the suburbs and city and county parks with arrows stuck in them (so rare that no reports are ever seen). Wounded deer go off and die a slow and painful death (even after the Camp Ripley wounding study showed extremely low wounding losses). Bowhunting is strictly recreational and plays no part in deer management (bowhunters take nearly 100,000 deer a year in Michigan, but that isn't management?).

We believe that the Archery Trade Association has the best take on all this. They note that the state wildlife agencies won't yield on bowhunting because the data are there to support the use of bows and arrows. State wildlife agencies support bowhunting. One tactic in stopping bowhunting is via the ballot box thru state ballot referenda. However, we do have a Ballot

Issues Coalition that responds to such initiatives with action and money. The members of this Coalition deserve your support and they are: the NRA, Safari Club International, The National Shooting Sports Foundation, the Archery Trade Association, the Congressional Sportsmen's Foundation, the Foundation For North American Wild Sheep, and several others.

There are things that every hunter can do. First, work to keep a positive relationship with your state wildlife agency. Your hunting clubs and state associations also need to keep in touch with state legislators, and you should be supporting the Ballot Issues Coalition members. One other positive thing to do is to start a National Archery in the Schools Program in every local public school (more on this in a minute). Yes, and why not work with agencies in your neighborhood and state to open bow and gun shooting ranges? Doing these things will force the HSUS-FFA merger to focus on something other than bowhunting.

Note, such mergers will continue making the dollars available to eliminate hunting much larger. For example, in 2006, the Humane Society of the United States merged with the Doris Day Animal League. Most of you have never heard of this organization, but they have major dollars that now go under the HSUS umbrella. More bad news.

Example # 3. It seems that every few months a new anti-hunting, anti-wildlife management crisis pops up in New Jersey. For example, every fall politicians guided by anti-hunters play havoc with much needed black bear hunts.

As bad as things appear in New Jersey, in July 2007 they got worse. Michael Panter, Democrat, sponsored Assembly Bill 3275 that changes the makeup of the N. J. Fish and Game Council. For decades the 11-member Council consisted of: two sportsmen each from South Jersey, Central Jersey and North Jersey; a farmer from each of those three regions; a conservationist; and an endangered and non-game species representative.

Now animal rightists are pushing for a bill that would allow the governor (no friend of hunting) to appoint seven people to the Commission. If a governor understands wildlife management and the values of hunting, then no problem. But what if he/she leans toward the animal rights side? Who might they appoint to the Fish and Game Council? Could this lead to the end of hunting in New Jersey? In the long run that is a possibility, but for sure if this becomes law, there will be many anti-hunting, anti-wildlife management decisions made in New Jersey.

You knew that politics were involved when this bill was directed to Panter's Environment and Solid Waste Committee rather than the Agricultural and Natural Resources Committee where it belonged. At the hearing in front of Panter's Committee, 40 people testified, and the committee voted for the bill. Supposedly changes will be made to the bill and it will be forwarded to the floor for a vote. One more thing. In the fall of 2007 the U.S. Sportsman's Alliance reported that this bill also directed the Commission to investigate non-lethal management options before setting hunting, fishing, or trapping programs. This bill would also transfer the Division of Fish and Wildlife from the Department of Conservation and Economic Development to the Department of Environmental Protection. If this bill passes, the head of Environmental Protection (no friend of hunting) would be making decisions on whether to allow non-lethal management before hunting seasons and bag limits are established. We've seen how such politics delays the bear hunting season in New Jersey. Can you imagine the disaster this bill and political approach would do to deer seasons, waterfowl seasons, etc.? What a nightmare.

Example # 4. The latest U. S. Fish and Wildlife Service survey (covers 2000-2005) shows that hunters aged 6-15 have increased by 4 percent, but overall, hunter numbers are down 10 percent. Some states have suffered more than others. Take Indiana for example. In 1996 there were 300,000 deer hunters in Indiana, but a short six years later that number plummeted to only 210,000. Top factors that influenced inactive Indiana hunters were "family obligations" and "loss of interest." Other factors were "personal health" (perhaps a reflection of an aging hunter population), "people violating game laws," "having to travel too far to hunt," "work obligations," and "cost of licenses." Factors that took away from the enjoyment of hunting were "game law violators," and "hunter crowding." "Cost of licenses," and "lack of private lands on which to hunt" were also factors that bothered Indiana deer hunters. What is happening in Indiana is typical of what is happening in many states.

Outdoor Uses of Wildlife is Big Business

True, hunter numbers are down, but other forms of outdoor recreation (e.g. hiking, camping, visiting parks, etc.) are also down. Before getting to the numbers, know that people love wildlife. I mean *people really love wildlife*. Consider that more than 71 million people 16 years old and older observed, fed, or photographed wildlife in 2006. They spent $45 billion (that's with a big B) to participate in these outdoor activities. Another 12½ million people 16 years old and older went hunting and spent $23 billion on trips, licenses, equipment, clothes, etc. Almost 30 million people 16 years and older went fishing. That's 13 percent of the United States population and they spent a cool $40 billion on their recreation in 2006.

These figures do not represent all wildlife users of the outdoors, just those who participated in 2006. Many more millions fish, hunt, and feed or watch wildlife, but they didn't participate for various reasons in 2006. And relative to fishing and hunting, these figures do not count the multi-millions of people who can hunt or fish on their own land without a license, or those 65 years and older who also don't need licenses in many states. These additions might well add another 25-35% to the use and economic figures listed for hunting and fishing.

Nonconsumptive wildlife activities such as feeding and photography continue to rise in popularity.

However good these figures sound, relative to the future of fishing and hunting, there is much to be concerned about. You see the numbers are down for 2006 when compared to 2001. For example, the number of anglers declined by 12 percent over the past five years. That number is down 15 percent compared to 1996. Fishing-related spending is also down, by 16 percent since 1996.

From 2000 to 2005 hunting participation dropped by four percent. The biggest drop was a 22 percent decline in migratory bird hunters, while big game hunters only dropped two percent. And all hunting is down by 10 percent since 1996. So, even though deer hunting is extremely popular, when we lose one percent per year, the handwriting is on the wall. Plain and simple, we are seeing a potential loss of 20 percent of hunters every 20 years.

Non-consumptive uses of wildlife are very popular in America and they have not declined. Fifty-six million people feed wildlife around their home, 19 million people photograph wildlife, and 13 million visited public parks or natural areas to see wildlife. And, as opposed to the decreases seen in fishing and hunting, there was an increase of eight percent in those who watch, feed, or photograph wildlife since 2001.

The decrease in spending for hunting and fishing is a concern because excise taxes on hunting and fishing equipment are a major source of funding of state wildlife and fish agencies. Consider that in 1996 fishermen spent $24.6 billion on equipment, but in 2006 that dropped to $17.9 billion. In 1996 hunters spend $14½ billion on equipment, but in 2006 that dropped to $10.3 million. While these decreases aren't huge, they only represent a 10-year period.

Even with these decreases in hunting and fishing, as I noted at the outset, people really love wildlife. As proof they spend around $120 billion a year to enjoy wildlife. Consider that there are more wildlife recreation participants in the country then there are mothers. It's true. Four of every 10 Americans participate in hunting, fishing, observing wildlife, feeding

Although the pursuit of a variety of species has fallen, deer hunting may be at an all-time high in some parts of the country.

The future of hunting depends on our ability to recruit new hunters.

wildlife, or photographing wildlife. Remember, this includes the millions in New York City or Los Angeles, or other huge cities who do not participate at all. Some may feed pigeons in the park, but most have no relationship with wild animals in any way.

The Hunter Replacement Ratio

As noted, hunter numbers are on the decline, and hunters are aging faster than the general population. But also note that the "hunter replacement ratio" (HRR) is below 1.0 in every state except Missouri.

What is the HRR and why is it important? Three years ago the National Wild Turkey Federation partnered with the U.S. Sportsmen's Alliance and the National Shooting Sports Foundation and released state Hunter Replacement Ratios (a simple measure of the number of youngsters coming into hunting compared to the old timers who died or dropped out). Most states showed ratios far less that the 1.0 needed to reach a break even point in hunter numbers. And nationwide for every 100 older hunters who passed away or stopped hunting, only 69 young hunters replaced them. Obviously, if this "hunter replacement ratio" (HRR) does not start to increase, hunting will slowly dwindle away, at least in the form we know today. In 2004 only seven states had HRR's above 1.0 and some of our biggest hunting states were well below 1.0.

The leading cause of low HRR's is restrictive hunting regulations, especially ones that do not allow kids to hunt until they reach age 12. There are so many activities for youths today, if they aren't hunting by age 12, they never will. Soccer, baseball, computer games, etc. will keep them out of the woods. We'll come back to this in a minute.

These low HRR's led to a "Families Afield" campaign to get states to lower their age 12 minimum hunting standard and make other changes that would encourage younger youths to take up hunting. In a short time "Families Afield" has made an impact.

For example, Pennsylvania passed a law allowing boys and girls less than 12 years of age to hunt if accompanied by a licensed adult. In Ohio youngsters can now hunt while completing their hunter education certification if accompanied by a licensed mentor. The National Shooting Sports Foundation notes that the states that were placed in the "family-restrictive" category, had 50% of all the hunters in the country, and the hunter replacement ratios in those states was way below 1.0. They are losing many more hunters than they gain. The good news is that many of those states are making changes.

In late 2007 the U. S. Sportsmen's Alliance, the National Wild Turkey Federation, and the National Shooting Sports Foundation announced that bills to reverse this downward spiral have been introduced in many states. Pennsylvania has 867,000 hunters, but a replacement ratio of only 0.62. They've passed a bill to allow new hunters to go into the woods under restricted circumstances before completing the state hunter education course. Michigan has 725,000 hunters, but also has the lowest replacement ratio in the nation at 0.26. Michigan passed two bills to help solve the problem. One lowered the age requirements for small game hunters from 12 to 10 years, and big game hunters from 14 to 12 years. The second did the same as the Pennsylvania proposal for kids before they are hunter education certified.

In fact, over the past two years 18 states have created less restrictive hunting regulations. Some made changes in when one takes the hunter education course, and others lowered the age when kids can hunt (with adult supervision of course). As noted above, some of the big hunting states to make changes were Michigan, Pennsylvania, Ohio, and Mississippi. Families Afield bills and regulations removing regulatory barriers including hunting age restrictions and hunter education mandates. Most exempted new hunters from hunter education for one year if they hunt under direct supervision of a licensed, adult mentor (usually the father). The latest state to do this was Kentucky, where they also revised the age when hunter education is mandatory from 10 years old to 12 years old.

Kids Want To Hunt

When I was a kid, living near a farm, all of my male friends hunted. Literally all. There was a relationship between rural life and hunting. In fact, there still is such a relationship. Growing up on a farm is a major factor

Hunting together as a family is not only a physically refreshing outdoor experience, it represents the ultimate resource of new hunters.

to determine whether a kid would hunt. Right below that is growing up in a rural area, but not living on a farm. And finally, if a kid who lives in a city spends time away from home in the country, that will be a positive influence on whether they want to hunt or not. Talk about a good reason to let your kids visit grandmother in the country during the summer. Obviously, rural life exposes kids to real life-and-death nature, something urban kids do not get, except via the boob tube.

What would it take to get more of our youth to go hunting? Fifty-six percent of youth said that they'd want to go hunting or hunt more if their father asked them to go. Fifty percent said they'd hunt or hunt more if a family member asked them to go; 49 percent if a friend asked them to go; 37 percent if mother asked them to go; 37 percent if they could learn more about guns (whoa, now we've scared some parents right out of their pants. The truth is that shooting guns at targets, at gun ranges, in competition, is just plain fun. It is done safely. Shouldn't we want kids to at least know gun safety?)

So, what are we missing here? Kids want to go hunting. Lots of kids, millions of kids, want to go hunting, and would go, if a family member would ask them to go. And for all you bow hunters out there, 35 percent of kids said they would go hunting or go hunting more if they knew how to shoot a bow. How hard is it to teach a kid to do something that kids love? Shoot a bow? And 35 percent would go hunting or hunt more if they could eat the meat. Hmmm....at a time when PETA is pushing vegetarian philosophy big time, trying to make kids feel guilty about eating meat, we have a huge number of our youth who want to eat wild game.

It has been said that since so many kids are raised in single-parent households, especially female-headed households, that this negatively affects hunting participation. Not so. In fact, kids from single-parent homes had just as high a chance to have hunted at some time than youths raised in dual-parent homes. In fact, children who lived primarily with their mother were more likely to have hunted in the previous year than were children

*Conducted under supervision, shooting sports are safer than many
of our more popular youthful activities such as football.*

According to Dr. James Applegate at Rutgers University,
68% of hunters who start before age 14 still hunt five years later
compared to 38% of those who started after 14.

who lived in dual-parent households.

Of those youths who said their parent(s) would not let them go hunting, the main reason was because parents felt it wasn't safe (42 %). The fact is that hunting is very safe. Safer than football by a ton. Safer than most forms of outdoor recreation. I guess it's just the gun thing that scares parents. Too much television, wars, street crimes, you name it.

But, the bottom line is that kids do hunt and they want to give it a try. Here is one other interesting tidbit. Those who tried fishing were much more likely to try hunting. Just another reason to take a kid fishing.

Why do kids like hunting? To have fun (85 %), to be close to nature (77 %) to be with family or friends (75 %), and for the challenge (72 %), the same reasons adults like to hunt. Kids who didn't hunt in the past year said it was because they did not want to kill animals (51 %), they just weren't interested (46 %), or they didn't have time (34 %, because of school activities and other hobbies).

Try Before You Buy

Even though kids want to hunt, many do not do so. One of the leading causes of the low number of kids coming into hunting is restrictive hunting regulation, especially regulations that do not allow kids to hunt until they are 12 years of age. The thinking is (and the truth is) by the time they reach 12, other activities have already cornered their interest.

As mentioned earlier, states with twelve or older minimum ages for hunters are at the bottom of the list relative to hunter replacement ratios. So, many of those states have changed that regulation. In addition, some have used the idea to let kids hunt under supervision before they take the hunter education course. The theory was that if you would allow a youngster the chance to try hunting before making a major investment in instructions and gear, more kids might hunt. Think about it. You take a new hunter turkey hunting. He/she sits in a blind and you call in a turkey. The new hunter shoots the turkey and that convinces them to continue hunting. Then they take the safety course, buy equipment, etc. As one game official in Vermont said, you "try before you buy."

Though this sounds like a good idea, there has been some opposition. In March there was an attempt to make such changes in South Dakota, but some hunter education instructors were opposed for safety reasons. However, data do not support this fear. Take Missouri as an example where youth can hunt small game, deer, or turkey without hunter education in the presence of an adult. In 1999, 4,775 youth participated. By 2006 there were 33,608 participants. But was it safe? Since the year 2000 there have been two hunting fatalities involving hunters under sixteen in Missouri, and both had taken the Hunter Education course. There were ten self inflicted non-fatal accidents, and all had taken the Hunter Education course. During that same time period there were no incidents where a non hunter education certified youth was the shooter.

We might add that between 2002 and 2006 there were 143 adults involved in accidents in Missouri and they all were hunter certified. Our point isn't that the hunter education course is not valuable because youths who took the course were involved in a few accidents. Hunter education courses are excellent and important, but even though a young hunter may not have taken an education course, when an adult supervises them, accidents do not occur.

Of 21 states surveyed where hunter education is not required for youths under 12 years of age, none felt that there were safety concerns. We're all for hunter education, but we need to reduce the barriers that prevent young people from hunting. There is nothing wrong with allowing youngsters to hunt with an adult for a short time, before requiring them to take the hunter education course. "Try before you buy," is a concept that is safe and brings more people into hunting. Hunter numbers are plummeting and we need to try new ideas that work.

Getting Kids Into The Shooting Sports

Hunting organizations have not been sitting on their thumbs and watching hunting slip away. There are a number of programs focused on getting kids into the shooting sports.

The National Archery in the Schools Program (NASP) is a prime example. As a young boy, I wasn't athletic, and because of my size, I was always one of the last to get chosen in pick-up football or basketball games. That didn't do much for my self esteem. My Little League baseball team won the championship, but I never played an inning (no coach could get away with that today). Needless to say, I didn't bother going out for Little League the next year. But at age twelve my dad bought me a Bear Grizzly bow, and things began to change. I could shoot that bow, and archery then led to bowhunting, something that was exciting, and something where I'd learn skills (patience, self worth, self reliance, nature study, etc.) that were useful throughout life. In fact, bowhunting led me to study wildlife, which then led me to be a wildlife professor and an outdoor writer. Both were, and are, fulfilling and exciting careers.

The point is that only certain youngsters have the ability to play certain sports, but shooting a bow is something any child can do. Short, tall, skinny, disabled; it doesn't matter. Anyone can shoot a bow and have fun doing it. With that in mind, and with the same Title IX problems (get more women into sports) in the public schools that have recently faced Universities all over the country, the Kentucky public school system started the "On Target For Life" archery program. Working with the state wildlife agency and the archery industry, a teacher training program was developed and implemented. In March 2002, an archery pilot program began in 25 schools and one year later they reached 121 schools and archery was off and running. Teacher support has been high because on days when archery is taught, school attendance is up. Classes are conducted indoors, there is no safety problem, and costs run about $2500 to get a program started in each school. Our archery industry has played a major role in the success of this program, but schools can also solicit help from local citizens and businesses. This is a win-win for everyone. Started in 21 public Kentucky schools in 2002, it has grown to 4,000 schools in at least 43 states (probably more now because new states are added almost every month). Eleven states have more than 100 schools involved, and 2.3 million kids have taken archery in their school since 2002. NASP expects another 750,000 kids to take the course in 2007-2008. When you consider that 27 percent of the students who took the course purchased their own archery equipment, you start to understand the potential for increasing the number of bowhunters via NASP.

And another 21 percent indicate they would like to bowhunt. When you consider that in a few years there will be one million kids a year learning to shoot bows, the potential for NASP to bring kids into hunting is huge. The key is to bridge the gap from the time they finish taking the class in their school to the time when they are in a tree stand.

Another great program is the National Shooting Sports Foundation's Scholastic Clay Target Program where female participation jumped 84 percent in 2005. This is a public school program where students shoot sporting clays. It turns out that women are really enjoying this program. Anti-gunners and anti-hunters won't want to hear this, but the truth is that more and more women are finding out that shooting guns in a supervised, safe way is just plain fun.

While some will wince at the thought of their daughters enjoying shooting guns, a survey of parents of girls in the Scholastic Clay Target Program showed that 94 percent believed it improved responsibility, teamwork, sportsmanship and leadership skills. Ninety-eight percent thought shooting was just as important as other school sports.

So, we have more and more girls shooting bows and guns and this

The Zaiglin girls demonstrate the fact that girls are every bit as good at hunting as boys.

shouldn't come as a surprise. The truth is that girls can shoot bows and guns just as good, if not better than boys. The reasons are that shooting a gun or a bow is not about strength, but more about coordination, concentration, and practice.

The fact that girls in the public schools are enjoying the shooting sports is part of a trend where more and more women are getting into hunting. You've got the Becoming an Outdoors Woman program and the National Wild Turkey Federation's Women in the Outdoors program. Women appreciating and enjoying hunting and the shooting sports is great thing for the sport as a whole.

If Not Hunting, What Are Kids Doing?

Even with all the above activity, we are still seeing a drop in overall hunter participation and although there has been an increase in the number of kids taking up hunting, that increase doesn't come close to replacing hunters who left hunting. Why? What else is going on here?

There were several papers presented at the Southeast Fish and Wildlife Conference held in West Virginia in the fall of 2007 that provided some answers as to why hunting is in trouble in America. Dr. Val Geist, retired Canadian wildlife professor discussed that hunting isn't part of our culture as it is in Europe. We have no songs, poems, plays, etc., showing hunting, while Europe does. (Remember the ditty, "A hunting we will go, a hunting we will go, Hi Ho amerio, a hunting we will go"). He noted that in Europe religion puts hunting forward by blessing the guns before the hunt, and having prayer stations in the woods. In addition, in Europe there is a ceremony to honor harvested game. Even the European military is linked to hunting, as the first snipers in uniform were German hunters. If hunting were more of our culture, as it is in Europe, perhaps more people would hunt, including kids.

In our country we have something called the Public Trust Doctrine. This means that the public owns wildlife in our country. Gordon Batchellor gave a paper noting that the erosion of this doctrine is leading to reduced hunting. There is more and more privatization of wildlife that leads to decreasing opportunities for hunting and an increase in elitists. In other words, for various reasons, hunting is inching away from being something all members of the public can afford to do. Privatization, commercialization and special interests are slowly but surely taking wildlife from the public trust. Thankfully the wildlife profession is very interested in keeping hunting under the Public Trust Doctrine, and they are looking at legal ways to strengthen this doctrine. Questions they are examining include public access, ownership of wildlife, and do state wildlife agencies supercede others in managing wildlife in their state.

Perhaps Gordon Robertson of the American Sportfishing Association presented the most interesting paper on why kids don't hunt. He noted that fishing (the same as hunting) declined by 12 percent in the past five years. That is a huge loss. Apparently kids aren't taking up fishing either. There's more. Bike riding is down 33 percent; waterskiing down 15 percent; and tennis down 10 percent. Most of these are family activities; things the family does together. As an aside, there were only two outdoor recreational activities that increased from 2000-2005. Golf was up 6 percent, and skateboarding was up 106 percent. Note that skateboarding is peer taught, not family taught.

Gordon listed four main reasons for the declines in outdoor sports: competition from indoor media, the fact that America is aging, fuel prices, and urbanization. Maybe that first reason is a key, because it reflects a tremendous competition for the time of kids 8-18. And so we're back to my original question. *Why don't kids hunt or fish?* Mr. Robertson offered these reasons. *How about the fact that they spend an average of 6½ hours a day on computers or watching television?* How about the fact that two-thirds have a television in their bedroom and half have video game players in their room?

Gordon goes on to state that fishing has tremendous value for kids maturing into adults. They learn a lot via fishing. We'd add the same goes for hunting. In fact, if parents fully understood the benefits kids get from hunting (and fishing), they'd make sure they all hunted. But it isn't happening. Other problems include access. But a real key is the fact that we aren't getting kids outside before the computers, play stations and television eats them up. That is why the effort to lower hunting ages is so critical. We don't care if a kid who hunts has a television in his room. We do care if that television keeps a kid out of the woods. We don't care if a kid who hunts plays video games, but we do care if video games keeps a kid out of the woods.

How can you help? Start your kid's interest in the field and streams at an early age. Take them on walks when you do your scouting. Take them for nature walks after church on Sunday. The key isn't to force them to hunt. The key is to expose them to the wonders of the woods before they discover the electric junk that captures their minds and leads to "nature deficit disorder." How important is doing this? The future of hunting depends on it.

Shed hunting is a great way to expose children to the outdoors. It's exciting and fun.

The future of hunting relies on our ability to pass the torch to our youth.

HUNTING HERITAGE AND HOW-TO

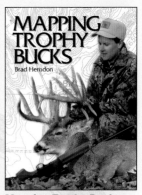

Go for Greater Understanding of Basic Deer Behavior

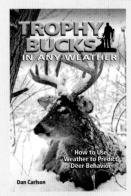

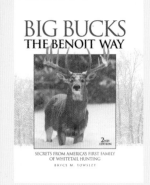

Trophy Bucks in Any Weather
How to Use Weather to Predict Deer Behavior
by Dan Carlson
This go-to guide for new and experienced hunters delivers biological and weather factors, including barometric pressure, fronts and air masses to predict deer behavior.
Softcover • 6 x 9
272 pages • 200+ color photos
Item# Z1781 • $21.99

Do-It-Yourself Dream Hunts
Plan Like An Outfitter and Hunt For Less
by Mike Schoby
Arrange an affordable first-rate hunt using tips for legally accessing private land, using public land, getting a tag, transporting meat and trophy home, and explore a state-by-state guide to license costs.
Softcover • 6 x 9
256 pages • 125 color photos
Item# Z1925 • $21.99

Big Bucks the Benoit Way
Secrets from America's First Family of Whitetail Hunting
2nd Edition
by Bryce M. Towsley
By following the legendary Benoit family, learn to track and harvest the biggest whitetail bucks. The full color photography and time tested methods explained will give you an advantage over whitetails and the bragging rights over deep camp.
Softcover • 8¼ x 10⅞
240 pages • 125 color photos
Item# Z2193 • $29.99

I Remember Papa Bear
The Untold Story of the Legendary Fred Bear Including His Secrets of Hunting
by Dick Lattimer
Discover pearls of wisdom from master outdoorsman Fred Bear as told through stories by his friends, including veteran rocker Ted Nugent.
Hardcover • 6 x 9 • 368 pages
125 b&w photos
Item# PPBR • $24.95

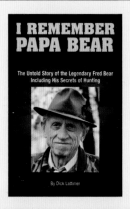

Hunting How-To and News at **www.deeranddeerhunting.com**